A DYER'S MANUAL

Jill Goodwin

A DYER'S MANUAL

PELHAM BOOKS
Stephen Greene Press

PELHAM BOOKS/Stephen Greene Press

Published by the Penguin Group
27 Wrights Lane, London W8 5TZ, England
Viking Penguin Inc., 40 West 23rd Street, New York, New York 10010, USA
The Stephen Greene Press Inc., 15 Muzzey Street, Lexington, Massachusetts 02173, USA

Penguin Books Australia Ltd, Ringwood, Victoria, Australia
Penguin Books Canada Ltd, 2801 John Street, Markham, Ontario, Canada L3R 1B4
Penguin Books (NZ) Ltd, 182-190 Wairau Road, Auckland 10, New Zealand

Penguin Books Ltd, Registered Offices: Harmondsworth, Middlesex, England

First published 1982 Reprinted 1985, 1990

Copyright © Jill Goodwin 1982

All rights reserved. Without limiting the rights under copyright reserved above, no part of this publication may be reproduced, stored in or introduced into a retrieval system, or transmitted, in any form or by any means (electronic, mechanical, photocopying, recording or otherwise), without the prior written permission of both the copyrights owner and the above publisher of this book.

Typeset by Rowland Phototypesetting Ltd, Bury St Edmunds, Suffolk
Printed and bound in Singapore

A CIP catalogue record for this book is available for the British Library

ISBN 0 7207 1327 7

ACKNOWLEDGEMENTS

I should like to express my thanks to the following who helped with this book by supplying illustrations, information, advice and/or encouragement: Rosemary Angel, Officer-in-charge, Museums Division, Royal Botanic Gardens, Kew; Jane L. Arthur, Curator and Librarian, Wisbech and Fenland Museum; Janet Backhouse, Assistant Keeper, Department of Manuscripts, British Library; David Baynes-Cope of the British Museum Research Laboratory; Jill Betts, Museum of Rural Life, Reading, who helped with flax hackles; the *Braintree and Witham Times*; D. J. Bryden, Assistant Keeper, Science Museum Laboratory; Josephine Darrah, Conservation Department, Victoria and Albert Museum; Judith Diment, Botany Librarian, British Museum of Natural History; Ray Harwood, photographer; Dr Robin Hill, who inspired continuous effort with woad and indigo; Dr F. E. Kenchington; Barbara Mortimer and Jenny Waterhouse of the Monega Art Centre, London Borough of Newham, whose class, held over a period of six weeks at my home, features in many of the photographs; R. S. Passmore of the British Wool Marketing Board; Jill Sanderson of Essex County Library, Chelmsford, who has tirelessly tracked down many an elusive book; the Shirley Institute, Manchester; Susan Slater, who typed the manuscript; Enid Tivey, who loaned wools, rugs, garments, dye samples and illustrations, and John Tivey who also loaned illustrations; Dr Werner of the British Museum Research Laboratory and Norman Wills of Long Sutton, Lincs, for their helpful correspondence on woad; Reginald Williams of the British Museum Department of Prints and Drawings; and the Librarians of Writtle Agricultural College, Chelmsford.

Finally I should like to thank, at Pelham Books, Ruth Baldwin who edited the text and Bob Eames who designed the book.

Contents

	Foreword	page	6
1	Introduction to Dyeing		7
2	Fibres for Dyeing		15
3	Equipment		29
4	Mordants		32
5	Test Dyeing		39
6	Dyeing with Weeds		44
7	Dyes from the Garden		47
8	Ancient Dyes		51
9	Indigo		67
10	Lichen Dyes		87
11	Dyeing in Schools		93
12	Using Dyed Fibres		100
	Dye Charts		106
	Metric Conversion Table		116
	List of Plants according to Colour Yielded		117
	List of Protected Plants		119
	List of Poisonous Plants		119
	Bibliography		120
	List of Suppliers, Museums and Craft Organizations		123
	Index		125

Foreword

Fortunately for the reader this handbook represents the extreme tip of a vast iceberg of notes and records on dyeing. Had I had a similar book at the start of my dyeing career, hundreds of hours and many mistakes might have been saved. But many days of delight and interest would also have been missed and it is to communicate some of the pleasure as well as the pains and frustrations of the experimental dyer that I have condensed and recorded the contents of my files.

We all influence each other, whether we like it or not, whether we realize it or not. So many people have had an unwitting hand in these pages. The chief have been my parents who provided a home background in which learning was encouraged; the men who worked for them on the farm; my dearly loved governess who showed us how to identify plants; and my botany tutor who taught me to question all things before accepting them.

Even greater help and encouragement has come from my husband Lewis, who has grown many of the dye plants mentioned in these pages and who has suffered without complaint (unlike Queen Elizabeth I) the 'Foul Oders' incidental to dyeing with woad and indigo. No one else would have evolved so many tactful ways of edging me towards the typewriter, or of suggesting means for storing an ever-increasing set of samples and paraphernalia.

The encouragement and interest of a very extended family is also important. Every author requires praise in large measure before criticism, and for me it has always been forthcoming.

The most helpful and curious coincidence came two years ago when a friend overheard me muttering that the only way to clarify a mass of almost unreadable notes would be to write a book and use them for the text. She said nothing, but within a week a prospective publisher was knocking on the door. So now, as we used to say in the nursery, read on.

Introduction to Dyeing

Colour is such a vital and vibrant ingredient of our existence that it is difficult to imagine what life would be like without it. The earliest-known use of colour by man dates back over 20,000 years to the caves of Altamira in Spain, where our ancestors used earth pigments like ochre as well as mineral ores for their paintings of bison, horses and other wild animals. The pictures, which are graphic in the extreme, have only survived because the atmospheric conditions in the caves prevented decomposition. With few exceptions textiles do not survive over such long periods, so that archaeologists have no way of knowing when man first began to use dyes for his fibres, but the oldest fragments of cloth belong to prehistory and are extremely ancient.

One such find, now to be seen in the Hermitage Museum in Leningrad, was made in 1947–9 by S. J. Rudenko, a Russian archaeologist, who discovered a beautiful rug in the Pazyrk valley in the Alti Mountains on the borders of South-West Mongolia and North-West China. The rug was found in the burial mound of a prince of Alti; grave robbers had broken into it soon after the interment and taken the precious metal and stones, leaving the rug behind. Freak weather followed and the chamber filled with water which then froze, leaving a deep-frozen rug until its discovery in this century. The rug was made c. 500 BC and had therefore been frozen for almost 2,500 years. Astonishingly, it was made with fine hand-knotting techniques and the vegetable dyes with which it was coloured survived the harsh weather conditions. It measures 6ft × 6ft 6ins.; the design of the border includes warriors on horseback, deer and winged horses, and the centre is composed of panels with a design of wings and tail feathers. This rug must be one of the greatest of archaeological discoveries ever made for it demonstrates the extreme antiquity of spinning, weaving and dyeing. To have achieved such excellence at such a remote period argues many centuries of cultural development leading to the finished product.

How then did early man discover the dyeing properties of plants, insects, minerals and soils? It was a long, slow process, full of trial and error, coincidence and chance. If only all the stages of discovery could have been recorded as they occurred we should have a priceless heritage on which to base our own experiments but, alas, written and pictorial records are comparatively few and many of them are incomplete, so that when following ancient methods and recipes modern dyers are not always successful in their results.

The new generation of dyers for whom this book is written, however, are tough and persevering, intelligent and educated, unlikely to abandon knotty problems without a struggle, and very different from those who practised the art of dyeing in the centuries before the Industrial Revolution. We have, too, vast reservoirs of technical knowledge in libraries and can draw on the assistance of experts in botany and chemistry for the answers to our unsolved questions. The motto 'Always go to the fountain head' should be pinned to the wall of every dyehouse and workroom.

This book is concerned with the natural colours we can make for ourselves from plants and insects,

Medieval dyers at work. (British Library. Royal MS 15E. iii, f269.)

and some soils, and the application of these colours to natural fibres such as wool, silk, linen, cotton, jute and nettle thread. No attempt has been made to deal with either synthetic dyes or fibres, for these present different problems and are beyond the scope of this book. However, with careful preparation some man-made fibres might be tried experimentally with the dye recipes given in later pages, though all will depend on the 'finish' of the yarns in question.

I have been dyeing with plants for over half a century and realize how little I know about many of the complicated reactions which take place in each dyebath as the work progresses. My bookshelves are lined with a great variety of tomes, all reflecting the experiences and conclusions of their authors. All are different; not one contains every dye plant or every shade or process of dyeing. On reading them it is manifest that the only certain thing about the use of natural dyes is the extreme uncertainty of the results. If we pause to wonder why this should be so the answer stares us in the face: unique material will vary with the soil and climate in which the plants are grown. To my mind the most useful and enjoyable books are those which admit to making mistakes (for most of my best discoveries have been made by error) and they are the ones most frequently read and propped against the dye saucepans.

Dyers, like other modern people, now move about the world to a degree undreamt of even a century ago. While writing, therefore, I have been mindful of the fact that my readers may travel and wish to use plants growing in countries other than their own. A basic system of extracting the colours from a plant is given in Chapter 5, 'Test Dyeing', and this method may be used with any plant in any part of the world. Some simple substitutes for the traditional mordants are also listed and even if they are not quite so effective they will at least keep the dyes from fading until more orthodox mordants can be obtained and applied.

Why do we use natural dyes at all when synthetic colours are fast, durable, and comparatively easy to apply? The answer lies in such places as the Victoria and Albert and the British Museums among the remarkable collection of textiles, particularly the rugs and carpets, where the visitor will notice that the rich and marvellous colours, all made before the discovery of aniline dyes in the middle of the nineteenth century, are as fresh and brilliant today as when they were first dyed and woven by nomadic people with primitive equipment. Many of the colours have been dyed in the fleece, not the hank, and laid in the sun to dry, so that the top wool may be several degrees lighter than the lower layers, and when it is finally spun as many as a dozen shades and gradations of one colour will show as bands in the yarn, the lighter tones catching the light and giving the effect of brilliance and lustre. Natural dyes are enhanced with age and only mellow into increasing beauty, whereas some aniline dyes fade with time into colours unlike the original.

In an era when the computer and multi-national company rule our lives it is interesting to note the immense revival of interest, over the last decade, in each of the ancient traditional crafts of pottery, basketry, woodwork and textile construction. Harassed by bureaucracy and the ugly products of the machine age, modern man appears to be turning more and more to making everyday objects for himself. Schools and adult education centres are full of students eager to use their hands, and spinning, weaving and dyeing are now among the most popular subjects among the classes available today.

Many people only arrive at dyeing as an adjunct to spinning and weaving. In fact large numbers of craftsmen begin by weaving, then find that homespun threads are much more interesting and rewarding to use, so they buy a spindle or spinning wheel to make for themselves the kinds of yarn they prefer. Finally they discover the beauty of natural colours and end by spinning, dyeing and weaving as a complete process.

Familiarity with one's raw material is the first necessity for any craftsman, and without realizing it at the time I was singularly fortunate in being born and reared on a remote farm in West Suffolk, where two flocks of pedigree Suffolk sheep were run in conjunction with other livestock. Before I started dyeing, spinning and weaving (in that order), I saw my raw material running about on the hoof and was taught to judge good and bad wool very early in life.

My first dyebath was made in 1923, when I was a child of six, from a plentiful supply of windfall damsons. With my two younger brothers I shared a governess who held us in thrall with a copy of *A Nursery History of England from the Early Britons to Queen Victoria*, with two pictures on each page, in full colour. The reds, blues, rusts and greens of Saxon and medieval England inspired us to experiment. Clothes in previous centuries seemed so much more colourful and exciting than our own country tweeds and covert cloths. Our ancient Tudor farmhouse had a large garden full of fruits, herbs and vegetables and provided plenty of raw material for our first essays in dyeing. We collected wool from daily visits to the sheep with our father and eventually had enough for the first attempt. The foremost problem was what to use as a dye saucepan. The mahogany tallboy by the sitting-room chimney had one corner piled high with empty Gold Block tobacco tins and these we removed and used over a small fire of sticks, in a retreat of our own at the top of the garden behind the huge summer house made of whole elm trunks and thatched with straw, a fine barrier and camouflage from the eyes of adults. Here many an unlikely brew was simmered. We were uninhibited and curious, ignorant of the first principles, but game enough to try anything on the chance of bright primary colours. Other ripe fruits followed the damsons into the tobacco tins and for several weeks we happily produced a number of bright pinks, blues and purples on our wool. Then quite suddenly, as children will, we went on to other delights, making dams and baking small bricks with the red local earth in our discarded dye tins.

But colour was immensely important to us as children, as it must also have been to primitive man, and the brighter and clearer the colours the better we liked them. Later when I left school and went on to an agricultural college I learnt how to fix the colours that I was still extracting in my spare time. Part of my course covered the study of botany and chemistry and this included mordants, the substances which dyers use to help colours adhere to fibres and make them fast to light and washing. My botany tutor was a remarkable man, well known for his work on the reclamation of sea coasts with *Spartina townsendii* (rice grass). He taught his students to persevere, never to give up, nor to believe anything until they had proved it for themselves. Nor were we to be afraid of making mistakes, for much could be learnt from them.

The approach of war in 1939 stimulated my already keen interest in textiles and I ordered my first spinning wheel at the Royal Show in Windsor Great Park in July. It arrived the day before war was declared, in a packing case shaped like a coffin, with minute instructions for its assembly and working. There was no spare petrol for journeys to evening classes so I had to sit down and teach myself to spin in the same way that I had learnt to make dyes, by doing it over and over again. By degrees the lumpy yarns became smoother and finer and many thick jerseys and pairs of socks were made to keep my family warm through the bleak war-time winters. These were mostly dyed with walnut husks, dock leaves, onion skins, indigo and dog's mercury, which produced shades of brown, green, gold, blue and buff respectively, all very harmonious when judiciously mixed and spun together after dyeing.

I soon found out that it was much easier to spin wool 'in the grease' – straight off the fleece – and to dye it in hanks rather than loose, but that if I wanted very subtle mixtures it was best to dye each colour and then blend the shades together by carding into a mixture before spinning. Some of the jerseys I made in those days are still in existence and are in themselves a strong argument in favour of the time and trouble spent in making them.

The dictionary definition of a philosopher is 'a lover of wisdom, formerly a student of natural science or of the occult'. Edward Bancroft, writing of dyes in 1813, aptly called his famous book *Experimental Researches Concerning the Philosophy of Permanent Colours*. In it he made known the conclusions that he had reached after many practical experiments with natural dyestuffs. Advanced as we are today, we still need to be philosophical to be happy and successful dyers – and I quite deliberately put happy before successful, for that is why most people use natural dyes. Like farmers, dyers are subject to natural laws and the ever-changing climate and periodically we tend to be cut down to size by outlandish weather conditions which may well negate previous experience.

The philosophy of the old Scottish dyers in the Highlands used to stress the importance of using as much as possible from nature. One in particular used to tell visitors to her croft that the beautiful blues she obtained for her tweeds were all achieved by using three raw materials, wool, indigo and stale urine for fermenting the dye, and that all three had an affinity for one another because they were natural substances.

Over the years all craftsmen evolve their own philosophy about their work. Mine has been influenced by the highly skilled men who worked on my father's farm. It was a large farm and there were thirty men and boys, all full of individual character. Obliged to be economical and frugal in their daily living because of their low wages, they brought a fine spirit of 'make do and mend' to their work. They would fashion tools for themselves from piles of metal and leather in the corners of the barns and stables. Instinctively my first reaction on needing a container for dyes, or a tool for spinning, dyeing or weaving is not 'Shall I buy it?' but 'Can I make it?' This attitude has led, among other things, to the home construction of bone and wood knitting and crochet pins, weaving shuttles and tapestry beaters, simple looms, and buttons and toggles for fastening homespun garments, carrying self-sufficiency a stage further from the sheep's back to our own without outside assistance or unnecessary expenditure.

In prehistoric times when man first began to leave his nomadic existence in favour of a more static and settled way of life in small communities, he experimented with many different kinds of fibre for clothing and household use, to replace the animal skins which he had formerly used for warmth and protection from the weather. This change took place very gradually over thousands of years and was geared to the development of netting, plaiting, knotting, spinning, weaving and knitting, as well as pottery and basketry. At the stage in civilization when a little leisure was left over from the daily struggle for existence, colour as decoration began to appear, and judging from my own experience as a child (possibly at the same level of mental development as adult primitive man) the earliest dyers would have noted the colours of fruits and vegetables when cooking them and would have tried to fix these colours on their yarns or cloth by heating in pots over their fires. How disappointed they must have been by their inability to fix so many of the promising reds and purples in roots and fruit.

In the great tribal migrations of mankind it is evident that not only tools, pottery and livestock were transported to new homes in new lands, but also the plants used for cooking, medicine and dyeing. In this way many plants have come to be removed from their natural habitat, but after a period of adjustment and modification have settled down and reproduced themselves successfully so that it is now quite difficult to assert where many of them originated. A case in point is woad (*Isatis tinctoria*), a plant which is indigenous to Assyria and the Eastern Mediterranean coasts, but which has been grown in Northern Europe for well over 2,000 years. In the twentieth century the transference of plants from one country to another has developed so that by means of land, sea and air transport we may now obtain and use dye plants from every corner of the world and even grow plants from other countries with a climate similar to our own. At the present moment I myself am growing four kinds of indigo-bearing plant in the farm garden, thanks to communication with dyers in other countries, whereas fifty years ago it would only have been possible to grow woad.

In prehistoric times many an enterprising soul must have perished through experiments with poisonous plants like hemlock, monkshood and deadly nightshade, and we owe a debt to these unsung heroes who first discovered whether plants were useful for food, medicine or dyeing (sometimes all three) and, if they survived, passed on

An illustration of 'garden woade' from the 1596 edition of Gerard's Herbal. *(Dr F. E. Kenchington.)*

their knowledge to their descendants. Even though separated by whole continents, groups of primitive people discovered ways of spinning, weaving, dyeing and making pottery and baskets; but our only guide to the origins of these crafts lies in archaeological remains, particularly over a wide area of the Far and Middle East as well as Egypt and Africa.

We know that in China dyers were at work over 5,000 years ago when Western Europe was relatively uncivilized, and that they were using plants, barks and insects as sources of colour. The Chinese developed a great silk industry a little later, based on the cultivation of the white mulberry (*Morus alba*) as food for the grub of the silkworm (*Bombyx mori*). In India cotton was used as the premier fibre while the Middle Eastern countries brought the dyeing and spinning of wool to a fine art. In Egypt hand-made linen, never surpassed in quality by the modern machine-manufactured variety, was produced for clothing and household use. The early peoples of each country simply used the fibres which were available and dyed them with plants which grew in their locality.

We shall never know by what chances primitive man discovered that salt, vinegar from fermenting fruits, natural alum and stale urine helped to fix and enhance the colours of his yarns, but for many centuries these four substances were used as mordants and they continued to be until recently in parts of the Scottish Highlands, among some tribes of American and Mexican Indians and in Central and South America, Africa and parts of Asia. The modern dyer using simple natural materials of this kind will be surprised how well his or her results compare with expensive chemical mordants, and in an emergency salt, vinegar and stale urine are still invaluable. Salt helps to fix dyes and prevent 'bleeding', vinegar improves all red and purple colours and dispels carbonates in hard water, and stale urine assists the fermentation and setting of all the indigo group whether of plant or laboratory source.

Over many millennia most of the common plants have been used or at least tried for dyeing. There are very few plants which yield no colour at all but, as most dyers have discovered, there is a preponderance of yellows, browns and fawns, fewer true greens, and remarkably few blues and reds. Early dyers worked empirically; slowly but surely they acquired a knowledge of dye plants, and passed on by word of mouth and finally by writing the wisdom of the years. The haphazard gathering of wild species gave way to the cultivation of the most valuable members of plant families for dyeing and until the middle of the nineteenth century the entire textile industry in every country depended on the harvesting of systematically grown dye plants in addition to others, like lichens, which were gathered locally from their natural habitat. In fact the growing of crops such as woad or madder in many European countries had considerable influence on the economy.

A Dyer's Manual is partly historical and partly an account of trials made with many plants growing in East Anglia, particularly in north-east Essex, with a rainfall of not much over 22ins. per annum. As rainfall and sunshine affect the concentration of colour in plants in any given year they must always be taken into account with each dye batch. Conditions will vary not only from parish to parish but also from farm to farm and even from field to field. A friend on a farm adjacent to ours has fields of heavy clay, whereas ours are either rich black river soil on the lower ground or hot dry soil on the higher fields. Between us we use plants from a wide range of soils and often obtain varying results from different corners of the farms.

It is the duty of the modern dyer to use plants which are plentiful and not endangered, to cultivate as many as possible for himself, and to press for the establishment in selected areas, such as the sides of motorways, of those plants which are native to that area and which have been displaced by roadworks. As we become increasingly aware of our place in the food chain we realize that the conservation of all species, whether plant or animal, may be imperative for our own survival. In Great Britain it is now against the law to uproot wild plants from the countryside, and harvesting of dye materials therefore requires care and thought. Permission should be sought from the owners of land on which plants are growing, if you wish to cut or pick a sample. Seed may be harvested in the late summer and then grown on in one's own garden. Never pick more than you need and always leave more than you pick, to seed. Lichens in particular should never be gathered to excess.

In cookery we have a school of thought which recommends the use of foods which are grown in the locality and which are plentiful and cheap. While this is too limiting a philosophy for most people today to follow to the letter and would certainly cut us off from much that is delectable, there is yet a grain of sense in it for novice dyers who might with profit concentrate their initial experiments on a series of so-called weeds growing in their own garden or immediate neighbourhood (see Chapter 6).

It is possible without any formal instruction to build up a wide knowledge of colours from plants by trial and error, and many dyers do so, but it saves time and money to study a group of plants before embarking on a large project. For many people, however, the very uncertainty of dyeing with natural material is part of its charm. The results from any given dyebath will differ from year to year with variations in sunshine, rainfall and the soil in which the plants are grown. This is itself an incentive to effort as well as a challenge to the ingenuity of the dyer, and the reason why all the quantities of both dyestuff and mordants given in this book are only to be used as a guide for further experiment and not as hard-and-fast recipes as for cooking.

There is no satisfaction to be compared with carrying out a primary process from beginning to end, the very thing which the Industrial Revolution checked and finally destroyed. The growing numbers of people who now rear and shear their own sheep and spin, dye and weave their own clothes and furnishings are in fact reverting to the days before 1750 AD. After many centuries of small-scale dyeing operations at home or in small dye houses by the side of streams, the scene changed dramatically in 1856 when W. H. Perkins discovered a violet dye from a coal-tar product, aniline, while he was engaged in research into a cheap substitute for quinine. Over the next thirty years the whole dyeing industry was revolutionized by great international chemical companies, who used his discoveries to widen the range to include all the colours of the spectrum.

Today, in our paints as well as in our dyes, we use the fruits of a century of research into colour.

Artists, however, are more concerned with the lasting integrity of their work than manufacturers and they cling tenaciously to methods which have proved satisfactory in the past. Among medieval craftsmen there was no desire for any of the 'built-in obsolescence' so prevalent today in many of our modern industries. At the end of the nineteenth century William Morris was the most notable example of an artist of this kind. Until his death in 1896 he championed a wide range of arts and crafts which included calligraphy, painting, and wallpaper and fabric design, as well as spinning, dyeing and weaving. After his death the art of dyeing with natural materials declined, and but for the work of a small group of dedicated craftsmen like Ethel and Philip Mairet, Violetta Thurstan, Elizabeth Peacock and Rita and Percy Beales who practised and taught spinning, dyeing and weaving in the decades after the First World War, we might have lost sight of centuries of carefully accumulated skills. To them and others like them we owe an enormous debt. It is always difficult to stand fast, as they did, in a tide flowing in the opposite direction, and they persevered in making beautiful and useful textiles when the majority of people bought and wore machine-made fabrics. But, though gradual in bearing fruit, their influence was enormous and all the best craftsmen today are their spiritual successors. Nobody reads their books or looks at their handwork without experiencing a desire to try the plants and recipes which they used so successfully. I first became aware of the work of twentieth-century dyers just before the Second World War, and the books which were available from them then have since been augmented by others written by their students.

When I first moved from Suffolk to Essex in 1945 there was not one other spinner or dyer in the area, but during the last twenty years the numbers have grown to such an extent that at a lawn spinning 'meet' in 1980 on this farm we entertained 115 spinners, dyers and weavers, nearly all of whom were using their own spinning wheels. Many of these guests were using wool from their own sheep, and those with white fleeces were anxious to use natural dyes. With this in mind I have tried in writing *A Dyer's Manual* to strike a balance between the reader who wishes to know not only how a certain colour is made but also why it is made in a particular way and the history of the process if it is very old, and the reader who wishes to plunge in headlong and achieve results without much preliminary reading.

Inevitably dyeing leads to an interest in botany, chemistry, soils, weather, and plant and animal husbandry, as well as in natural fibres of all kinds. In Great Britain we have as wide a selection of pure and crossbred sheep as any country in the world, and for this reason the prospective dyer tends to concentrate initially on wool as it is cheaper and easier to acquire than either cotton, linen or silk, all of which require more preparation before dyeing can begin. However, there are choice spirits who delight in testing out tough plant leaves, or unusual kinds of animal fur, to see if they will not only spin successfully but take up dye as well. In Chapter 2 I touch on a few of the most common and widely used fibres, but the list of these is not encyclopaedic and the reader should not be deterred from making his or her own experiments.

My own philosophy of dyeing, which has evolved over the past half-century, may be summarized as follows:

1. You are using unique materials, therefore the result, whatever it may be, will be unique; no one else will make exactly the same colour.
2. It does not matter in the least whatever any pundit may say about the colour you ought to achieve from these plants; what really matters is that you are making an effort on your own to find out more about *all* plants.
3. It does not matter if you blunder into error and make many mistakes, for a great deal is to be learnt from failing. One is forced to consider a great many factors in the success of each dyebath.
4. Only use the results of other people as a rough guide, for their conditions will not be the same as your own. Prove everything by your own efforts.
5. Share experiences and results with others because you may act as catalysts for each other and spark off fresh lines of thought.
6. Never be discouraged by apparent failure but go back and think carefully over each stage of the dyeing, considering the soil, season, sunshine and rainfall.
7. If one mordant fails to give a good result, try all the others in turn, and combinations of them if necessary, to see if a better colour will result.
8. Persevere with each problem, for sometimes after years of thought the solution will become clear.

Fibres for Dyeing 2

Wool

Wool is the first choice of the dyer, spinner and weaver in the British Isles, for it is easily available and relatively cheap compared with other fibres, most of which have to be imported. For this reason the recipes throughout this book refer mainly to wool.

Before beginning work a wood turner or potter considers his raw material very carefully and the textile craftsman must do likewise, comparing the relative merits of the different types of fleece just as he would the various kinds of silk, cotton, linen and other animal and vegetable fibres. Dyers are concerned with the way in which fibres absorb colour, either before or after spinning them. In the case of wool, there is a great deal of difference between the ways in which even the coarse and fine types take up colour.

Britain has a variable climate and our clothing needs to be able to 'breathe' in cold and damp. Wool is the premier fibre for insulation and as it has taken millions of years to evolve it seems unlikely that it will ever be surpassed by man-made fibres. Capable of absorbing over thirty per cent of its own weight in moisture, wool will generate heat while it is wet and still keep you warm. In hot weather garments made from wool will absorb body moisture to a far greater degree than cotton, silk or linen and will also keep the heat *out*.

In Great Britain we are fortunate in having upwards of fifty pure or crossbreeds of sheep from which to select fleece. The quality, softness and length of staple, i.e. fibre length, which each of these provides vary considerably according to breed. It is well worth making a preliminary study of several different fleece types before deciding which to buy.

British sheep fall into three categories:

1. Mountain, e.g. Herdwick, Blackface;
2. Downland, e.g. Southdown, Suffolk;
3. Long-woolled, e.g. Lincoln Longwool, Wensleydale, Leicester.

These categories are composed of breeds which have evolved over the centuries in certain areas to meet local needs, and their characteristics have become fixed and permanent. The little Cotswold sheep supplied the medieval wool trade and the Scotch Blackface was used for making hard-wearing carpets. Nowadays one is as likely to see the Suffolk sheep in the Lake District or Scotland as the local Herdwick or Mountain breeds which were once the only ones found in those areas. From the dyer's point of view all the breeds of sheep are of interest as the fleeces from them take up dye in slightly different ways, the short, softer wool of the downland breeds being particularly absorbent of colour and requiring less time and lower temperatures in the dyebath than longer-stapled and coarser wools. It is in the long-term interest of all who work with wool to join the Rare Breeds Survival Trust, thus helping to preserve some of the rare sheep breeds from extinction. Even if we cannot all keep a few sheep ourselves we may help others to do so and thus provide a useful 'gene bank' for future generations.

It is possible to buy wool either 'in the grease' or washed and sorted. Wool may be obtained in the

Fine examples of the various types of British sheep: above left, rough fell (mountain); above right, Lincoln Longwool (long-woolled); below, Suffolk and Southdown (downland). (British Wool Marketing Board/Douglas Low.)

grease from several different sources, particularly now that so many people keep a few sheep in their paddocks or orchards for their own and family spinning. Farm parks and zoos are also useful places in which to look for not only wool but also camel, yak, llama hair and mohair. The under coat of these animals provides soft fibres suitable for dyeing and this needs to be separated from the hairy outer coat or carded carefully before spinning.

In the British Isles, however, the main supplier of wool is the British Wool Marketing Board (see the list of addresses at the back of this book), who publish an excellent handbook listing all the types of fleece which they provide together with the current year's prices for the different breeds and qualities of wool.

The price of wool is rising rapidly with general inflation. Gone forever are the days when 1lb of wool would fetch 3 shillings in a good year. In 1974 the average price per lb was 26p to the grower and the price to the buyer after grading and handling costs would have been double this figure. At the time of writing the price of wool varies between 50p and 400p per kilo (2.2lb). There are indications that the ceiling may have been reached, but the spinner must remember that the price of raw wool is usually no more per lb than one pays for 1oz of manufactured wool so that, even allowing for loss of weight in washing and dyeing, wool is still a bargain fibre.

Personally I like to see my wool 'on the hoof' before I buy it, and note the size, weight, age and health of the sheep before it is sheared. It is possible to return year after year for the same fleece from the same sheep if you know the owner and he knows your likes and dislikes, for sheep run in commercial flocks live for seven or eight years and those which are kept in smaller units often flourish until they are fifteen or sixteen years old. Sheep have been bred by many members of my family, including three who were 'improvers' of the Norfolk Horn, the Southdown and the Suffolk breeds. All were concerned with improving the weight, texture and quality of their wool as well as the mutton of their chosen breed. Invariably they found that good wool and good mutton go hand in hand.

Wool may be bought ready washed and sorted either from the Wool Marketing Board or from one of their depots, or from craft shops. Most dyers buy their wool 'in the grease', however, and sort their own fleece before storing it, as wool in this state repels moths better. Inevitably there is a loss of from a third to a half in weight when wool is washed free of dirt and grease and this should be taken into account when calculating the quantities required for a particular project. It pays to buy the cleanest, best-quality wool to avoid waste.

Wool varies not only with the breed of sheep but also with the soil and conditions under which the flock has been kept. The cleanest fleeces come from sheep which have been running on chalky soils or high downland pastures or on the very light dry soils of East Anglia, particularly Norfolk.

It is fascinating to spend a day watching the shearing of a flock of sheep and every spinner and dyer should do so if it all possible. As the fleeces fall to the ground they will be seen to vary enormously: some will be heavy, clean, healthy-looking and of superb quality; those from sheep which have been ill will be light and the wool tufts will break when they are tweaked sharply with the fingers — these are fleeces to be avoided.

As a child and adolescent I used to catch the sheep for the shearers and eventually was allowed to turn the handle of the manually operated clippers. Time is precious to the shepherd with a flock of several hundred to be sheared, and it was only recently that I had the opportunity of joining a two-day shearing course for agricultural trainees and learnt the New Zealand method by which an expert shearer rhythmically removes the fleece in just over two minutes. By handling over two hundred fleeces after shearing it was quite easy to select the twenty best by weight and texture alone, as they fell on the barn floor from the upward

A Derbyshire gritstone fleece immediately after shearing. (Monega Art Centre.)

17

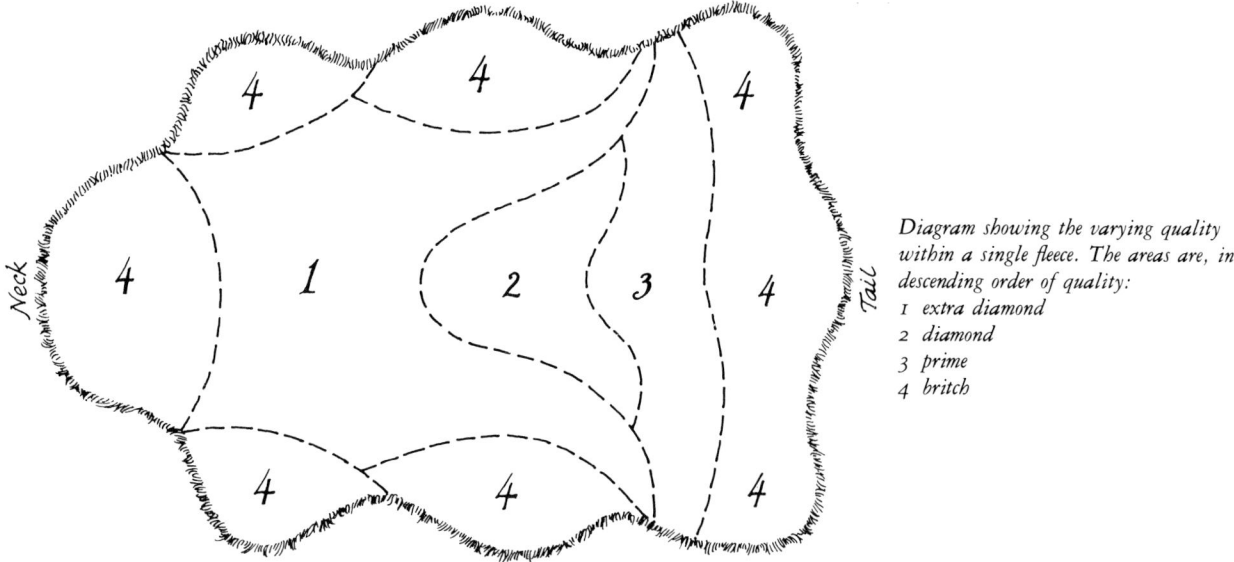

Diagram showing the varying quality within a single fleece. The areas are, in descending order of quality:
1 extra diamond
2 diamond
3 prime
4 britch

throw which the packers give to flatten the fleece before rolling it and tying it by the neck wool ready for the woolsack.

In its wild and prehistoric state the sheep had a coating of rough outside hair and an inner coating of soft wool, and in existing primitive breeds this double layer may still be found. But centuries of selective breeding have reduced the hair content and increased the wool, an important development from the dyer's point of view as the hair and kemp in wool resists dye absorption. For uniform results a high-quality fleece is desirable.

It is important for dyers to know the basic structure of different kinds of fleece so that they may be handled correctly and with the minimum amount of damage. One strand of wool consists of an outer layer or cuticle with a tiny set of scales from root to tip which shed moisture away from the sheep's body. Inside the cuticle is a cellular structure of protein called the cortex: in coarser wools this has an air space (the medulla) in the centre but it is absent in finer wools. Every fibre has tiny waves known as 'crimps' and these vary from a few in long, coarse wool to many per inch in the fine wools.

Wool is classified by the ability by which it may be spun finely. The 'count' system is based on the fact that, for example, 1 lb of best Southdown wool can be spun into 60 skeins of a standard 560 yds each, the British maximum. A count of 60 and above is internationally called 'merino', a synonym for high quality, while a count of below 44 indicates a wool in the carpet category.

Sheep of the three longwool breeds, Lincoln, Leicester and Wensleydale, all grow wool in curly locks which must be pulled apart and washed before they can be spun. It is well nigh impossible to take up a freshly shorn fleece of any of these breeds and spin it before washing and dyeing, as one can with that of most other breeds. Until a century ago and the advent of heavy industrial machinery, fearsome iron combs were used to reduce the long wools to long 'slivers' which were then spun into fine, hard, worsted thread.

The best way in which to see a great variety of fleeces at one time and obtain expert advice on the handling quality of each kind of wool is to pay a visit to the headquarters of the British Wool Marketing Board.

The International Wool Secretariat is also a

useful source of information on supplies of wool from other countries, and local wool growers depots exist in Kent, Herefordshire, Wales, Oxfordshire, Northumberland and in Scotland. The Agricultural Advisory Service in each county will give information on local flocks of sheep.

County agricultural shows, the Rare Breeds Survival Trust and county craft fairs are all places where fleeces may be seen and studied. In 1978 a revival of the original sheep shearing of 1778 was staged at Holkham Hall in Norfolk. Also on display were pens of rare breeds of sheep and cattle, old farm machinery and large marquees filled with local spinners, dyers and weavers. This two-day event was justly popular and provided an excellent opportunity for the public to see wool on the sheep's back being sheared and converted into yarn which was then dyed, spun and woven. A coat made in a day was also on view among many fine examples of knitting, crochet, rugs and weaving.

A similar exhibition of self-sufficiency took place at the Essex Show in 1979 and attracted enormous interest. It was quite evident that the general public as well as prospective craftsmen considered the return to hand spinning, dyeing and weaving an economic proposition. Such dem-

Three examples of spinning wheel: above left, a fine 25½in.-diameter ash wheel by Jim Hennequen; above right, a table model of a great wheel made by Enid Tivey (base and upright of beech); below, a Scandinavian-type 23in.-diameter wheel by Frank Herring & Son. (John Tivey.)

onstrations now occur frequently in each county and are worth looking for.

There are two kinds of spinners and dyers and

they approach their raw material in different ways. The first will take endless trouble to search out the type of fleece he requires, with a definite end in view. He will sort the fleece carefully into several grades and either use them separately or card them carefully together so that the whole fleece is roughly the same texture throughout. He will then wash and dye the spun yarn before making it into the garment or piece of cloth that he has in mind. The second craftsman will buy whatever wool is nearest to hand, wash, dye and spin it, or spin, wash and dye it if he likes spinning in the grease, and will only decide what to make with it when the yarn is coloured. Both methods have their advantages as a trial of each will show. The second and more haphazard method opens up vast possibilities in subtle colour combination before spinning begins, but the grease in unwashed wool makes it far easier to spin and novices are therefore advised to spin first and dye after washing and hanking the yarn.

PREPARATION OF WOOL FOR DYEING

Sheep have sebaceous glands which secrete a greasy, water-soluble wax (from which lanolin is made), and sweat glands which produce a substance known as suint. Combined together these make the 'yolk'. The finer the wool the greater the quantity of yolk in each fleece. Long-stapled coarse wools contain far less grease, a fact which must be borne in mind when washing wool before dyeing. The amount of grease in wool is also dependent on the climate in which the sheep was reared. Those kept by the Navajo Indians of Arizona living under desert conditions produce extremely clean wool which requires only shaking and teasing before dyeing: their fleeces are not as oily as those from sheep reared in cold, wet climates. In the British Isles, sheep's wool is full of oil which acts as a natural waterproof against the high rainfall. This must be carefully removed before dyeing can begin as it repels dye. The majority of dye baths which fail to 'take' are due to imperfect removal of the grease in the wool.

The first stage of preparation for dyeing therefore is to wash the fleece very thoroughly to remove every scrap of grease or dirt to allow the dye to 'bite'. Large quantities of soft rainwater are ideal and a downpipe from the roof to a water butt will provide a good supply. I am lucky in having a 600 gallon ship's boiler outside my kitchen door which gives soft water for washing and dyeing as well as for precious garden plants in hot, dry, summer weather. Melted snow, lake and stream water can also be used, but as a last resort use Calgon, vinegar or ammonia to soften hard tap water.

One of the best cleaners and conditioners for really dirty wool is stale human urine, kept for a fortnight in a closed container such as a big plastic bucket with a well-fitting lid to allow the ammonia to develop. There is nothing to touch it for leaving the wool in fine, soft condition for dyeing or as a conditioner after dyeing to counteract the harshening effects of mordants such as ferrous sulphate or stannous chloride. The urine, which was used extensively in the Bradford blanket trade until very recent times, is easily washed out of the wool with several rinses. Few modern dye books mention urine, which is free and easily available to everybody, either as a cleansing agent before dyeing or as a ferment for woad, indigo and some of the lichens which yield reds on fermentation. All the older generation of dyers used urine extensively, as they still do in the Scottish Highlands, in parts of America where early colonial skills have been carefully preserved, and in Africa, India and South America where indigo is still fermented in the ancient manner.

To Scour Clean Wool for Dyeing
Heat soft water to hand heat. Add one cupful of liquid detergent (e.g. Stergene) per gallon and whisk to a froth. Gently add the fleece and leave to soak for one hour. Lift and drain the wool carefully without squeezing. Repeat the process with cooler water until the dirt has been removed. Rinse in tepid soft water until all traces of lather have disappeared.

To Scour Dirty Wool for Dyeing
Place the fleece or yarn in sufficient cold soft water to cover it and leave for twelve hours to penetrate thoroughly and loosen the dirt. Gently lift the wool from the water and drain, then lay it in a bath of tepid soft water containing a liquid detergent. Really dirty fleeces need one to three days' soaking; cleaner ones a few hours. The dirtiest fleeces I have ever washed came from three Icelandic sheep which had been running in a peat bog. Each fleece required a week's soaking and ten separate washes, and even then fragments of peat fell into my lap as I was spinning.

Spinning wool should never be shocked with extremes of temperature or it will 'felt'.

To Make Felt
If you wish to make felt for hats or clothing you simply do all the things to wool which you should not do when preparing it for ordinary spinning and dyeing. Card or tease 1 lb of wool into thin layers and place them across each other in bands of at least seven or eight layers deep, in a large bowl or sink. Sprinkle the wool with pure soap flakes and

A demonstration of the felt-making process. (Monega Art Centre.)

then pour on very hot water, followed by very cold water, pounding the wool between each soak with a wooden mallet. The wool will then contract sharply to make a dense layer which on drying out will cut like material. Lightweight and beautifully soft hats may be made by cutting the felt into circles and shaping them round a pudding basin with the steam from an electric kettle. If the water level in the kettle is below the spout the steam will emerge as a really powerful jet and will be most effective as an aid to shaping. Felt can only be dry cleaned, so it is best to use it for objects which do not need to be washed.

To Dry Wool

Wait for a blowy, sunny day, wash the wool and then spread it on clean grass or old sheeting if it is still in the fleece, or on the washing line if it is in hanks. Never store wool until it is completely dry or it will become musty. If mordanting is to follow washing, the wool is used damp from the last rinse.

Silk

Silk is available to the dyer in several forms, direct from the cocoon, or as sliver, yarn or silk waste. Unlike wool, silk is a luxury fibre because of the high cost of production. It should be treated with care and respect as it is sensitive to alkalis and requires neutral or acid dyebaths if the fibres are to remain in good condition. Many dyers prefer to use natural dyes for silk as they do not injure the fibroin or insoluble protein of each filament and because natural dyes have as great an affinity for silk as for wool.

The Chinese developed the art of rearing silkworms over 4,000 years ago, mainly from the moth of *Bombyx mori*. The silkworm, the grub of this moth, feeds exclusively on the leaves of the white mulberry, *Morus alba*. Several other wild or half-wild silkworms such as Atlas, Eri, Muga, or Tussah which feed on castor-oil plants or oak leaves are found in India and Japan and provide additional supplies. Today silk farmers rear large numbers of worms each year on the leaves of carefully pruned Mulberry trees. In the twenty-five days from hatching to pupation the silkworm increases its weight by ten thousand times and eats voraciously, converting more than seventy per cent of its intake of nitrogen into silk substance. The silkworm has two glands filled with a concentrated solution of fibroin and sericin, which unite in the spinnaret, a small hole in the muzzle of the worm. The extruded silk coagulates in air and after attaching the first fibres to straw or branches for support the worm deposits many layers of silk round itself to form a cocoon. If the cocoons are required for breeding they are allowed to hatch into moths, which mate and lay eggs for the next life cycle. The cocoons required for silk are stifled by heat and the silk is then wound off into a continuous filament, several strands at a time for strength. This is a skilful and delicate process, but in Japan much of the silk is now reeled on automatic machines.

Either raw silk (reeled silk, thrown silk or drawn silk) and waste or spun silk are the forms in which silk may be bought. Raw silk is covered in gum which must be boiled off in a soap solution before dyeing can begin. Waste or spun silk is mordanted and then dyed, as for wool.

DE-GUMMING SILK

The silk is first made into skeins and tied loosely in four or five places as it expands greatly when wet. It is then immersed and boiled in a strong soapy solution made with 2–2½ gals of water to every ½lb of silk and sufficient neutral or olive oil soap to make a good lather. The solution is brought to the boil and held at simmering point for 1–1½ hours. After rinsing the silk may be mordanted and dyed while it is still wet, or carefully dried and stored. Dried, scoured silk should always be

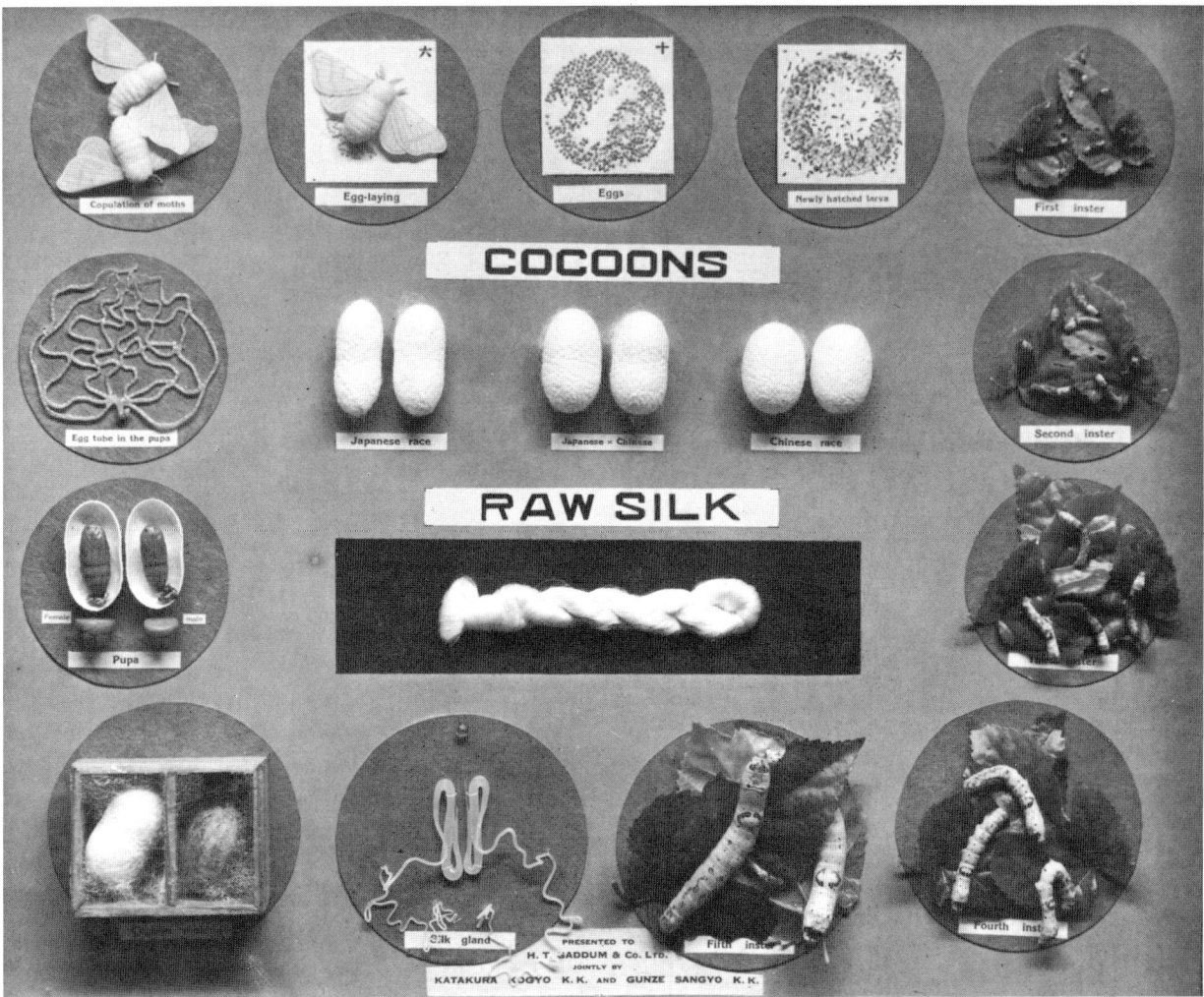

The life-cycle of the silk worm. (Shirley Institute.)

thoroughly 'wetted out' before mordanting and dyeing. At the present time the greatest demand is for woven silk, but it is a versatile fibre and it may also be knitted or crocheted, or spun fairly thickly like fine wool and woven on hand looms to make material similar to middle-weight wool cloth.

Very warm underclothing as well as jerseys and caps can be made from a mixture of silk and wool which has been plyed together and then knitted. Silk fabric should always be washed by hand with neutral or olive oil soap, and squeezed gently without rubbing or wringing out. Mild liquid detergents may also be used in moderation. Silk is best dried slowly and pressed on the wrong side of the fabric with a warm iron while it is still slightly damp.

TO MORDANT SILK

Allow 4 gals of water for 1lb of raw silk.

1. Use an enamel or stainless-steel pot for mordanting and dyeing.
2. Tie the silk carefully in four or five places to prevent tangling.

Breaking flax.

Hackling.

Scutching. (Ray Harwood.)

become as fine as human hair.

Spinners in olden times used to say that flax should be kept in a dry place and hackled often. Undoubtedly it is much easier to break when it is bone dry and I always make sure that mine is laid by the Aga cooker overnight until the stems feel quite brittle.

TO SCOUR LINEN

To enable full dye absorption, linen should first be scoured. Heat 3 gals of soft water and make a rich lather with pure soap suds. Add 2 tablespoons of washing soda. Lay the hanks of linen in the water and boil for two hours. Cool in the water and then rinse out all the soap. Dry and store the fibres or mordant them while wet from scouring.

TO MORDANT LINEN

    1lb dry linen fibres
    3 gals warm soft water
    4 oz alum
    2 tablespoons washing soda

Heat the water with the dissolved mordant and add the linen. Boil for one to two hours – if the flax is fine, boil for one hour; if coarse, for two hours. Cool the fibres in the liquid. Rinse and

The author spinning flax; breaking is in progress in the background. (Braintree and Witham Times.)

either use for dyeing immediately or dry for storage.

DYEING FLAX

Several plant dyes are unsuitable for flax, but many barks, sticks and oak apples give good colours, as do indigo and woad. I always put a small sample of silk and linen in my wool dyebaths to see what effect will be produced. If you keep records of all your experiments you will be able to build up a useful file for future reference.

Other Animal and Vegetable Fibres

In every country of the world there are plants and animals which produce fibres which can be twisted and spun into threads for dyeing. The general rule when dealing with a new and unfamiliar fibre is to treat all the animal fibres as if they were wool and all the plant fibres as if they were flax or cotton.

Animals whose hair can be used are as follows:

1. All the goat-like descendants of the camel such as the alpaca, llama and vicuna which are to be found in South America and in wildlife parks and zoos in this country.
2. Tibetan goats, which give Kashmir wool.
3. Angora goats from Asia Minor, which provide mohair.
4. Angora and other long-haired breeds of rabbit.
5. Any dog or cat with hair 3ins long.
6. Tibetan yak – rather coarse but very strong hair.
7. Musk ox, otherwise known as quivit. There are two coats, one of hair and the other of soft wool, which must be separated before spinning.
8. Camel, single- or double-humped species. The hair from the latter produces the best fibres. Again there are two coats which should be kept separate, the inner soft wool being the best. The outer hairy coat makes up into very tight, strong threads.

All the animal fibres listed above spin more easily with the addition of a little oil to the fingers, as they will have been washed before spinning begins. Use a mixture of one part olive oil, one part distilled or boiled water and one part ammonia, well shaken together.

Some of the more unusual vegetable fibres which can be spun are:

Agave sisalana (sisal)
Agave fourcroydes (henequen)
Phormium tenax (New Zealand flax)

The above three plants all give coarse strong fibres from their leaves and require damping before spinning, like ordinary flax. They should be treated like flax when mordanting and dyeing.

Other useful plants are:

Corchorus capsularis, Corchorus olitorius (jute)
Cannabis sativa (hemp)
Urticaceae species (nettles)
Boehmeria tenacissema, Boehmeria nivea (rhea or china grass, collectively known as ramie. Produces a white silky fibre obtainable in rovings which can be spun like worsted. The thread from ramie is not very elastic but it is very strong).

All the bast fibres given above are prepared in a similar manner as flax.

Equipment 3

Dyeing equipment varies with the dyer, but a large container, a soft water supply, a source of heat and some dye material are the most basic requirements. We all have favourite cooking pots and gardening tools, and so it is with dyeing: the tools and pans, stirring rods, spoons and other paraphernalia soon become dear to us for their particular purpose.

As many of the mordants used for dyeing are poisonous, the dye saucepans should *never* be used for cooking. Saucepans which look completely different from the household collection are preferable. Farm sales and auction rooms are fruitful fields for the dyer hunting for containers, and large strong saucepans may be picked up at bargain prices. House-clearance specialists often offer a wide range of shapes and sizes very cheaply. If you are buying enamel pans they must be unchipped, for if rust is present it will affect your dye colours as it has the same effect as the mordant ferrous sulphate. White enamel linings are of course the best for showing up dye colours. Ideally, however, saucepans should be made of stainless steel as this will affect the colours least of all because it will not chip or rust. Copper, brass or iron pots will all modify colours as will aluminium, particularly if soda is added to the dyebath.

Use stirring rods made from glass, peeled hardwoods, old wooden spoons, or best of all from stainless steel (made from fine tubing). A hook on the end of the rod will prevent it from slipping into the brew.

I never now use weighing scales for plant materials as experience has taught me that it is useless to do so: I may need twice the quantity of dyestuff to produce the depth of colour in a wet year as would be necessary in a hot, dry season. Scales are useful for weighing mordants, but experience will soon teach you to measure in spoonfuls or by eye, like an expert cook.

A drying line out of doors is useful for skeins of yarn, and old sheets or blankets may be spread on the lawn for drying fleece or fibres.

A notebook is vital if you are going to do a lot of dyeing for you will quickly forget your dye source, time of picking, soaking, mordant and simmering time if you do not record them at once.

To make storage boards for dye samples, saw a

The author showing how to use a dye sample board. (Monega Art Centre.)

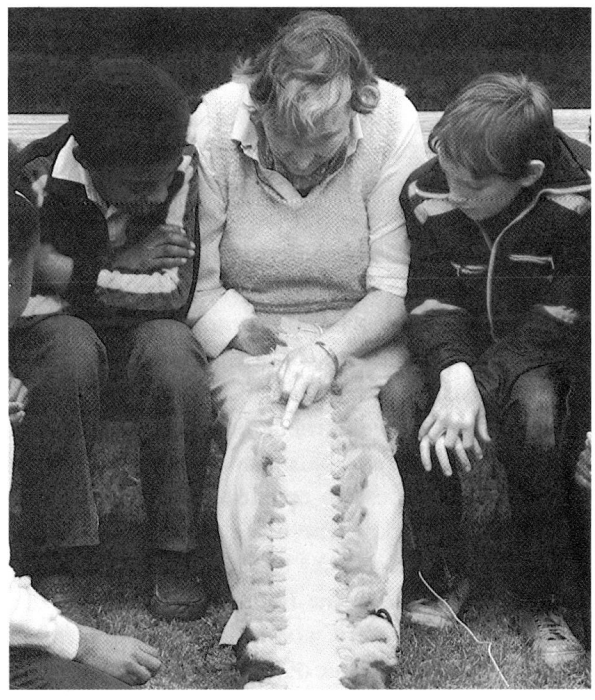

4 Mordants

Natural dyes are either substantive, needing no mordant, or adjective, requiring one. Without mordants many dyes would fade badly or 'bleed' when they are rinsed, but originally, until this was realized, primitive man boiled his plant material to extract the colour and simmered his yarns in the resulting liquid, and when the colours faded he repeated the process.

The word mordant comes from the Latin verb meaning 'to bite'. Early French dyers were among the first to discover and use certain metallic salts as mordants. They considered that the salts made the fibres rough and porous and better able to absorb the colour from the dyebath. Today we know that mordants have an affinity for both fibres and dye material and improve the fastness of even substantive dyes.

A mordant may be used:

1. On washed, damp yarn or fibre before dyeing.
2. In the dyebath while the dye is being simmered.
3. After dyeing with the plant material.
4. Before *and* after dyeing, for extra fastness.

In these days of rising inflation the cost of dyeing is always in my mind, for with all but a very few dye plants a mordant is necessary if a really permanent colour is to be obtained, and mordants are becoming increasingly expensive. Plants which contain tannin need little, if any, mordant when used for dyeing, and to trace them two classic books are of inestimable value. The first is *The Concise British Flora* by W. Keble Martin, MA, FLS, for visual identification of the plant in the field; the second is *A Modern Herbal* by Mrs Grieve, FRHS, edited by Mrs Leyel. Equipped with these two peerless volumes the dyer is able to track down a wealth of information about plants.

Any plant with *tinctoria* as part of its Latin name will yield a dye, and additional pointers are those containing tannin and having a strong smell. Using the *Flora* one might select *Isatis tinctoria* for blue, *Rubia tinctoria* for red, and *Serratula tinctoria* for yellow. With the *Herbal* the *Cruciferae* and chamomile families, both with pungent scent, would suggest themselves as candidates for the dyepot.

In previous centuries the following substances have all been used as mordants and they may be employed with equal success today:

Wood ash, in solution
Stale urine (at least two weeks old)
Salt
Vinegar
Sorrel roots
Sumach
Oak galls
Raw alum
water in which rusty iron has been soaked
Willow or oak bark
Copper filings or pieces soaked for two weeks in ammonia (for blues)

Wood-ash liquor was one of the substances much employed by early dyers for obtaining fast blues with woad and indigo. Instructions for making it are given in the section on woad in Chapter 9, page 83. It must never be used to excess when used with wool as too much will harshen or even rot the fibre.

A vibrant selection of dyed unspun wool samples, the colours obtained from plants ranging from lichen to woad. (Ray Harwood.)

All the mordants used for dyeing should be clearly labelled 'POISON: DANGER' and kept in a safe place well out of the reach of children.

When we consider the instructions and recipes in old dye manuals we must remember that the practice of mordanting *before* dyeing may have been evolved to suit communities dealing with large batches of yarn, fleece or cloth who wished to divide the operations into specialist departments. The earliest dyers of all had few cooking pots and little water, especially in desert areas, so they combined their operations to use as little liquid as possible. Thus the Navajo Indians who inhabit the desert regions of North America still wash and dye their wool in one pot of water simultaneously, and fortunately their fleeces are free of grease and dirt.

The main mordants used for natural dyeing today are as follows:

Alum (potassium aluminium sulphate). White powder.
Copper sulphate. Blue, poisonous crystals.
Bichromate or dichromate of potash (chrome). Poisonous orange crystals.
Ferrous sulphate (copperas). Green crystals.
Stannous chloride. White tin crystals.
Tannic (gallotannic) acid. Buff powder
Oxalic acid. Poisonous white powder.
Washing soda (hydrated sodium carbonate). White crystals.
Pearl ash (purified potash).
Cream of tartar. Used to modify the harshening effects of some of the mordants. Soft white powder.
Salt.
Ammonia. Colourless liquid.

Most dyers use only alum, copper, chrome and iron, though even these are not easy to obtain from ordinary chemists. Tannic acid, oxalic acid and stannous chloride have to be ordered from specialist dye firms which often take months to deliver small orders, so be sure to contact them well in advance. Time can sometimes be saved by bulk ordering through your spinners' and weavers' group.

I have concentrated mainly on wool in this chapter because, as previously stated, it is the most popular fibre among home dyers today.

General Instructions for Mordanting Wool

1. Allow at least 1gal water for 4oz wool.
2. Be sure that the saucepan is large enough to hold both wool and water.
3. Have ready either carefully tied hanks of yarn or loosely teased washed fleece, damp from rinsing.
4. Tie the hanks loosely to allow the mordant to penetrate thoroughly. Only stir the wool occasionally while mordanting or it will felt.
5. Dissolve the mordant in a little boiling water. Stir until dissolved, then add to the saucepan of tepid water. Add the wool and simmer gently for half to three-quarters of an hour for soft wool, one to one and a half hours for coarser wool.
6. Drain the wool; do not wring but squeeze gently. If the wool is to be stored for later use, rinse and dry it; if not, use immediately while still damp.
7. *Always* wear rubber gloves for mordanting as many of the mordants are toxic.

USING ALUM

This is the most generally used of all the mordants, usually in combination with cream of tartar (4oz to 1oz cream of tartar), which is included to brighten the colours and keep the wool soft. Too much alum makes wool sticky.

Allow 3–4oz alum per 1lb of wool, rather less for fine wool. Dissolve the alum and cream of tartar in a little boiling water and add to the rest of the water, stir well and heat for five minutes. Add the clean wet wool and bring to simmering point, taking an hour to do so. Keep at simmering point for forty-five minutes to one hour, stirring gently from time to time. Cool for fifteen minutes and drain the wool. Either use it immediately or dry it and store in a clean cotton bag.

USING BICHROMATE OF POTASH

This is a comparatively recent mordant, unknown to dyers a century ago, but very easy and effective to use, leaving the wool soft to the touch. The orange crystals are sensitive to light and should be stored in dark bottles. For this reason the saucepan should also be covered while mordanting is in progress, and the wool stored in the dark afterwards until it is required for dyeing. Bichromate of potash is an excellent mordant for orange and red dyes and enhances the colours from onion skins, cochineal, flowers from many plants of the *Compositae* family, and certain wild fruits and leaves. As well as being very effective for wool, it is also good for silk. Use the following recipe.

> 4oz wool
> 1gal soft water
> ⅛oz or scant ½ teaspoon bichromate of potash

1. Put the bichromate of potash in a little boiling soft water and stir well until dissolved. For some plants 1 teaspoon of cream of tartar will improve the colours.
2. Add the clean wet wool and weight it with a small plate or saucer to keep it submerged.
3. Cover the saucepan and simmer gently for an hour, stirring occasionally.
4. Cool the saucepan; drain and squeeze the wool. Because bichromate of potash is so sensitive to light it is best to mordant with it immediately before dyeing, remembering to keep a lid on the saucepan during both operations.

For yellow and orange flower heads I find it best to dye and mordant simultaneously as flowers need only minimal simmering. To do this dissolve the bichromate of potash in boiling water and add to the saucepan of flower heads which should have been previously soaked in cold water. Add the wool, cover the pan, bring to simmering point and simmer for one hour. This method produces brilliant oranges from fresh or dried onion skins if a pinch of stannous chloride is also added halfway through the hour of simmering.

USING COPPER SULPHATE

Use gloves when handling copper sulphate as the crystals are poisonous, and be particularly careful to prevent cuts or sores from coming into contact with it. Alone in water, copper sulphate imparts a bluish-green colour to wool; moss green if soda is added. It is an unpredictable mordant and is capable of producing very fine greens with some plants and of changing others into bronze, khaki or olive shades, depending on whether the plant juice is acid or alkaline. One summer when I was dyeing with dandelion flowers the dyebath containing the copper sulphate and the plant juice turned a deep indigo blue when a few drops of ammonia were added. I thought that I had discovered a new source of blue dye, but this outstanding colour slowly faded on simmering and settled down to a fine moss green.

With acid plants of the *Rumex* genus, such as dock or sorrel, copper sulphate will give fine shades of bronze; with mullein, elder leaves, toadflax, comfrey and many other thick-leaved plants, a wide range of deep greens.

If other mordants fail to produce good colours from a plant it is always worth trying copper sulphate alone or in combination with ferrous sulphate, the latter being added about fifteen minutes before the end of the dyeing time. Cream of tartar added to the other two mordants helps to keep the wool soft and to brighten the colours. Use the following recipe:

8oz wool
2gals soft water
2 teaspoons cream of tartar
½oz or 4 teaspoons copper sulphate crystals

1. Dissolve the copper sulphate and cream of tartar in hot water and add to the saucepan of water.
2. Add the clean wet wool and simmer half an hour for fine soft wool, one to one and a half hours for coarser wool.
3. Drain the wool, squeeze gently, and use at once or store when dry for future use.

USING FERROUS SULPHATE

Ferrous sulphate may either be bought as fine green crystals or prepared by dissolving scrap iron in dilute sulphuric acid and allowing the solution to crystallize.

Iron was used as a mordant for wool and cotton from early times but it has a hardening effect on fibres and tends to darken and 'sadden' colours, so it must be used with care. In small amounts and with certain plants, iron will give outstanding greens. With rhododendron leaves it gives good grey shades and on many plants it has a modifying effect. The recipe is:

8oz wool
2 teaspoons ferrous sulphate
1 teaspoon cream of tartar
2gals water

1. Dye the wool in the plant liquor by simmering for forty minutes to an hour.
2. Dissolve the ferrous sulphate and cream of tartar in a little hot soft water or some of the hot dye liquid and add to the saucepan after first lifting the wool out.
3. Stir well and gently replace the wool. Do not stir but simmer very gently for fifteen minutes.
4. Drain and rinse in soft water to which either 2 pints of stale urine or a cupful of vinegar has been added.
5. Wash and rinse very thoroughly.

USING STANNOUS CHLORIDE

This is useful as a modifying agent with other mordants. It has a brightening effect on colours, particularly on reds and oranges, but it must be used in small quantities only, and with great care, as it tends to harden wool and make it brittle. If the wool is to be mordanted before dyeing it should be put into a bath containing a *cold* solution of stannous chloride and either oxalic acid or cream of tartar. The temperature of the bath is then raised to simmering point and held for an hour.

The recipe is:

8oz wool
1½ teaspoons stannous chloride
2 teaspoons cream of tartar *or* 1½ teaspoons oxalic acid

When tin is used with other mordants as a brightening agent it is first dissolved in hot water and then added to the dyebath for the last twenty or thirty minutes of simmering. Rinsing should always be extremely thorough after dyeing. I find that stannous chloride alone will produce the most brilliant oranges from simmered onion skins and that no other mordant is required. Indeed the merest pinch will be sufficient. With madder too the results are excellent.

USING TANNIC ACID

Tannic acid is much used as a mordant for brown and buff dyes, and wool dyed with it tends to darken with age. Some plants contain natural tannin, including oak, elder and sumach, and many of them give good fast colours on their own without other mordants. Tannic acid is a useful mordant for cotton, silk and linen as well as for wool.

Skeins of wool richly dyed with woad, lichen and elder leaves. (Ray Harwood.)

Willows contain tannin and the brown and buff colours of basket willows are obtained by boiling the bundles of cut osiers for up to four hours in a large tank. On stripping and peeling, the colour will be seen to have penetrated to the white core of the rods and dyed them fast. For wool, willow bark peeled and used as a dye will give bright pinks from some soils. If large concentrations of bark are used the colour will become deep rosy pink and will be fast. Use the following recipe:

8oz wool
3 teaspoons tannic acid
1gal soft water

1. Dissolve the tannic acid in hot water.
2. Add to the saucepan of water and stir well.
3. Add the wet wool and simmer for one hour.
4. Leave the wool in the bath until it is cold.

USING OXALIC ACID

This is a useful mordant for fixing blues, purples and pinks from fruit dyes. It may be bought as a powder from chemists and should always be stored out of the reach of children and marked 'POISON'. Oxalic acid occurs naturally in both garden and wood sorrel, which may be used instead of the powdered form. Another useful and safe source of oxalic acid is the 2ins of rhubarb stalk nearest the ground which may be cut off and used when the rhubarb is harvested for eating.

Many dyers believe that oxalic acid will give better colours if the mordanted wool is stored in the dark for a few weeks before being dyed. The recipe for using oxalic acid is:

8oz wool
2 teaspoons oxalic acid
1gal soft water

1. Dissolve the oxalic acid in hot water.
2. Add to the saucepan of cold water.
3. Add the clean wet wool and simmer for one hour.
4. Rinse well.

Possible Snags in Mordanting

1. Too much ferrous sulphate will make wool hard and rough.
2. Too much bichromate of potash darkens wool.
3. Too much tin will make wool brittle.
4. Too much alum will make wool sticky.
5. Too much stirring will felt wool.
6. Badly dissolved mordants will produce patchy and blotchy yarns.
7. Badly tied yarns will come undone and give endless trouble.
8. Skeins which have been tied too tightly will have undyed patches under the ties.

Double-check your mordant weights. Look twice at your yarn ties. Never stir wool vigorously in the mordant or dyepot, but always move it very gently.

Mordanting After Dyeing

Mordanting is usually carried out before dyeing but there are occasions when this is not possible, for example when you suddenly wish to test an unfamiliar plant and have no ready-mordanted wool available. As a test the plant may be simmered simultaneously with the mordant and wool to see if there is enough colour to justify further investigation. Only long practice and much experience will teach you the plants which may always be used for simultaneous mordanting and dyeing.

Mordants for Silk

If you produce your own silk it must first be degummed by boiling in soap. Allow 2oz soap to ½lb of silk and boil for at least one hour.

Alum is the principal mordant for silk and should be used as follows:

1lb silk
3oz alum
3gals soft water
1oz carbonate of soda crystals

1. Dissolve the alum and soda in the water.
2. Stir well and steep the silk in the mixture overnight.
3. Wash the mordanted silk well before dyeing.

Test Dyeing 5

The wisest course in dealing with unknown plants or other dye material is to use only small quantities of fibre or yarn and try out a tiny sample of each plant for colour. This will save time and fuel for you may find that the colours obtained are not worth using in larger batches. Keep a few really small saucepans or tiny frying pans for test dyeing: pint-sized containers are quite large enough. Small vacuum flasks kept only for dyes are also invaluable.

Each season different weather conditions will cause dyeing results to vary quite considerably, so it is important to record the sunshine and rainfall leading up to the harvesting of the plant in question though it isn't necessary to go into more detail than 'dry and sunny', 'wet', or 'very wet'. Soil conditions should also be recorded and any other influencing factors which might affect each dyebath.

The vast majority of modern spinners who dye their own yarns use wool, but it is always interesting to include a small quantity of silk, linen, cotton or any other fibres you have to hand when you are test dyeing and in this way you will build up a useful reference chart of samples for future experiments with larger amounts if you discover that a particular plant is very good. Many plants will dye silk, wool and linen as well as cotton, and some form of identification is obviously necessary when several kinds of yarn or fibre are dyed together. Some dyers use a system of knots; others use buttons or toggles made of wood or bone. It is less confusing always to use the same identification for each mordant or fibre, e.g. mordant: alum – one knot; wool – one button or toggle; mordant: copper sulphate – two knots; linen – two buttons, etc.

The secret of successful test dyeing lies in recording details with care and precision, for results will vary from year to year and only by comparing the work of several seasons will a pattern emerge. Hot dry summers, for example, invariably produce brighter colours than cold or wet. Use strong labels and *indelible* ink and attach the labels immediately the yarns or fibres are dried from dyeing. One thing is very certain: if you do not record your results you will very quickly forget how you obtained them. When dyeing is in full swing in my kitchen and as many as four plants are being used at a time with different mordants for each plant, I write all the labels out before beginning operations and attach them immediately the yarn leaves the dyepot. Strips of plastic and indelible laundry markers are useful for labelling wet yarn.

In this book Latin as well as common names of plants are given as an aid to identification in any country in which they occur. Confronted with an unfamiliar plant one must ask several questions:

1. Is this plant poisonous or benign? (If poisonous, use rubber gloves in handling it.)
2. Do I know the plant family to which it belongs?
3. If I do, have I used any other plants from this family, and if so what colours did I obtain from them?
4. Did I use stems, leaves, seeds, flowers, roots or the whole plant?
5. Has this plant an acid or alkali bias? (If acid I am likely to get additional colours from it by using

ammonia as an afterbath.)

6. Does this plant contain any natural tannin? If it does, I shall not need much, if any, mordant. (Remember that **Mrs Grieve's** *Herbal* gives plants' tannin content.)

7. What time of the year will this plant be at its best for dyeing?

8. Will this plant be best if used fresh, or will it dry and still give good colours after storage?

By considering these factors many problems may be eliminated at the outset before dyeing actually begins.

We are living in a time of great change when all the long-established natural dyestuffs such as indigo, madder, and cochineal are becoming scarce and very expensive. It is important therefore that we should allow full rein to our curiosity and test all the available plants in our own localities. Many plants which are never mentioned in standard textbooks yield excellent colours: some of them are hated weeds like pepperwort (*Lepidium campestre*) or cleavers (*Galium aparine*); others, such as forsythia, grow in most gardens.

After some practice and experience we may wish to go further afield in our own or other countries to see whether there are similarities between plant families, or whether soil and climate in other areas produce variations. Once we have evolved a standard testing procedure it may be used in any part of the world and with any dye plant. Many craftsmen now travel, and no opportunity should ever be missed of exploring the dye plants of other lands.

Many plants such as docks, sorrel, weld, comfrey and flowers of the *Compositae* family give as good or better colours dried as when they are fresh because they are concentrated when dried and rubbed down to a powder. Drying racks are easily made from old picture frames covered in cotton sheeting and on these nuts, shells, flowers and leaves may be dried like herbs in a warm current of air (e.g. in an airing cupboard, hanging in a warm kitchen or even in a very cool oven). Once dried the material is best stored in porous containers such as cotton pillow cases or large paper bags. I use strong potato sacks made of several layers of brown paper. It would be fatal to use plastic bags as there is always a danger of moulds and fermentation. Dried dyestuffs need frequent checking however they may be stored.

With hard material such as tree bark, nut shells, shrub prunings and plant roots a soaking of four to five weeks in soft water before dyeing will result in deeper colours. For some barks and for woods and sawdust of cedar and redwood, a cupful of rubbing alcohol or vinegar added to the soaking water will help to extract more colour and give deeper shades.

Plant dyes are acid or alkaline, rarely neutral. Each may be tested with litmus paper and the results noted for future reference. Acid dyes from red and black fruits like damsons, blackberries, sloes, elderberries or raspberries will all be enhanced with the addition of vinegar. If ammonia is added to make them alkaline, the colours will all shift from red to green.

Rather than white fleeces, many spinners and weavers prefer to use coloured fleeces ranging from pale grey to dark chocolate black in their natural state, but interesting effects may be produced by

Skeins of wool dyed with woad (centre), and the lichen Parmelia saxatilis *(right), with an undyed skein for comparison. (Monega Art Centre.)*

Rugs and cushions made by various techniques with home-dyed wool. (Ray Harwood.)

over-dyeing some of the paler shades with stronger colours and it is worth including small samples of various coloured fleeces with each dyebath that you make. Grey wools over-dye well with oranges.

Levelling

When dye lots are similar but not exactly matching it is possible to 'level' them by simmering in a bath of hot water containing Glaubers Salts. Allow a half cupful of Glaubers Salts for every 8oz of wool or yarn. Dissolve the salts in warm water and add the wet yarns. Add enough water to cover and simmer for thirty minutes to one hour, longer if the colour shades are very different. Rinse the fibres and hang to dry in the shade.

Equipment for Test Dyeing

Before starting work, check that you have the following items:

1. Small saucepans of stainless steel, unchipped enamel or glass.
2. Small vacuum flasks, or a hay box.
3. Sieves, and strainers made from old nylon tights or stockings.
4. Bamboo, glass or stainless-steel stirring rods.
5. Mordants.
6. Chinagraph pen or indelible pencil.
7. Stiff card or waterproof labels made from thick plastic.
8. Supply of soft water for simmering, washing and rinsing.
9. Board for storing dyed samples (see page 29 for how to make this).
10. Strongly bound book or file for a complete record of every process.
11. Dye thermometer.
12. Sea salt and ammonia for afterbaths.

Methods of Test Dyeing

Test dyeing may be done using either the saucepan or vacuum flask/haybox method.

SAUCEPAN METHOD

1. Simmer the prepared dye material very gently, with enough water to cover, for one hour.
2. Cool for an hour and strain, using the liquid as the dyebath.
3. Establish the acidity or alkalinity of the liquid by testing with litmus paper. Red litmus paper turns blue in an alkali; blue litmus paper turns red in an acid.
4. Add the pre-mordanted fibre.
5. Simmer for one hour. Cool.
6. Rinse in cold salt water.
7. Wash, rinse and dry.

The author leads a class on an expedition to gather water-side plants for test dyeing. (Monega Art Centre.)

6 Dyeing with Weeds

Dyers in every country of the world have always retained an affection for so-called 'weeds' as they are among the most useful sources of colour and they may be used in the dyepot with a clear conscience. What is a weed? Farmers all agree that a weed is any wild plant which appears in their fields in competition with the crops they are trying to grow. Add to this a dreadful motto heard in East Anglia, 'If it runs, shoot it; if it grows, spray it', and you have modern farm psychology in a nutshell. Light is beginning to dawn, however. Research is now going on into the uses of some of the oldest-known farm weeds as controls for cereal pests, and within a decade we may be encouraging back the very plants that we have been trying to eradicate for over half a century.

When harvesting weeds for dyeing, other than your own, it is best to adhere to the old rule 'only decimate', i.e. take one in ten, and always leave more than you gather. In the British Isles it will be interesting to note the changes in weed population which are bound to occur now that rural councils are financially unable to mow the roadside verges. Species of weeds which suffered by being cut before they could seed are found to be increasing once more.

As already mentioned, a very useful guide to the detection of colour sources in plants is scent. Remember that any plant with a pungent smell is likely to give good strong colours, for example walnuts (all parts of the tree as well as the green husks of the ripe nuts), dahlia flowers, onion skins, ragwort, tansy, toadflax, woad, horseradish leaves, pepperwort, lesser burdock and dandelion flowers, to name but a few.

Sometimes the members of a particular plant family will yield a similar range of colours. The *Compositae* (daisy) family is an outstanding example, for nearly all the flower heads, fresh or dried, will give yellows or oranges with alum and cream of tartar or bichromate of potash as the mordant, and with copper sulphate a fine range of greens. The dye is found in the flower stamens, not in the petals as one would suppose, so that whatever colour the flowers, whether they be golden dandelions, blue chicory flowers or purple thistles, the colour in the dyebath will always be yellow. In *The Concise British Flora* W. Keble Martin lists over 120 native members of the *Compositae*, some of which occur in every county in the British Isles. At least a dozen are therefore available throughout the dyeing season, beginning with daisies and dandelions and continuing through the summer to fleabane, tansy and ragwort.

If you are weeding in the garden never consign a likely weed to the compost heap without a test: surprising results may be frequent. From the hedgerow blackberry leaves and shoots give a wonderful colour range of blue-green to black with copper or ferrous sulphate, and elder leaves give excellent greens with these two mordants. Bracken at all stages of its development from fiddlehead to mature plant in August is a useful source of greens and browns. Dog's mercury in the early spring and nettles between late February and October both yield green and brown – the older the leaves, the longer the plants need to ferment in soft water before simmering.

The *Polygonaceae* family includes bindweed, knotgrass, bistort, common and water persicaria

A collection of beautifully coloured wools dyed with woad, indigo, madder, walnuts and willow. (Ray Harwood.)

A knitted hat of Romney Marsh wool, with undyed stripes alternating with stripes of plied wool dyed with woad, ripe elderberries and persicaria leaves. (John Tivey.)

cabbage leaves with alum and cream of tartar, but the colours are not as bright or as fast as those from woad or indigo.

Roots

Allow at least twice the weight of roots to that of the fibre to be dyed. Soak the roots for three to seven days according to toughness and then simmer gently – all members of the madder family should be simmered *well below* boiling point. Remember that roots vary greatly in the speed with which they release their colour.

Beetroot is the obvious candidate for the dyepot but disconcertingly yields rather ordinary soft yellow and peach shades. A better red comes from our old garden enemy cleavers or goosegrass (*Galium aparine*) which ramps along our flower borders in June and July. This is the best time for harvesting as the whole plant can be dug and the tough brick-red bottom roots – not the fine ones attached to the plant stems – can be cut off and used after a good wash.

Shrub Prunings

Allow twice the weight of chopped plant material to the weight of fibre you wish to dye. Prunings should be soaked in soft water for a week or longer, depending on their toughness. After soaking they should be simmered slowly for several hours and then strained and the liquor used as the dyebath.

Rose, sumach, berberis, apple, walnut, pear, birch and nut prunings are all useful sources of pinks, browns, buffs and yellows. All woody dye material gives better colours if 1 tablespoon of vinegar is added to each batch while soaking.

Fruits

Allow twice the weight of fruit to the weight of fibre to be dyed. Soak the fruit for twelve to forty-eight hours in soft water – the riper the fruit, the more quickly it will break down. Simmer gently for one hour. Strain, and use the liquor as the dyebath.

You will find that the dye colours produced are similar to those of the fruit themselves but lighter. With all the red, pink, purple or black fruits, 1 tablespoon of oxalic acid, acetic acid or vinegar

Woollen bags and hats dyed with colours from plants and a woad-dyed felt hat (centre), displayed with a mat made from nettles dyed with elderberries (on side of basket) and, underneath that, a mat of plumber's hemp. (Ray Harwood.)

added to the simmering bath will improve the colour. If ammonia is added to fruit dyes all the colours shift from reds to green.

Vegetables

Allow twice the weight of plant material to the weight of fibre to be dyed. Soak the vegetable for twelve hours, simmer for one hour, strain, and use the liquor as the dyebath.

Some vegetables which are useful for dyeing are: salsify, carrot tops, fennel leaves, sorrel leaves, beetroot (though see under 'Roots' in this chapter for comments on the unexpected colour produced), and tomato vines.

Nuts and Seeds

It is preferable to avoid using seeds for dyeing as the practice can be wasteful of the following year's crop, but sometimes there may be a surplus of certain varieties when it is possible to experiment with a few small lots of seeds to see what colours can be gained.

Allow twice the weight of plant material to that of the fibre to be dyed. Soak according to ripeness and hardness – soft seeds require only one day's soaking, hard shell cases a week – then simmer gently. Walnuts in particular give deeper colours with very long soaking, but they need to be simmered up frequently during the soaking period to prevent moulds from forming on the surface. Walnuts produce the most outstanding nut dye, though the entire walnut tree – twigs, catkins, bark, small dropped nuts and the mature nut shells – may be used for a wide range of browns from coffee to nearly black. I always try to harvest my walnuts into an opaque container as the colours seem to be affected by sunlight. The catkins in particular should be used immediately after harvesting to avoid loss of colour.

Alder fruits also give good pinky browns on simmering after soaking for several hours.

Sunflower seeds give blues with alum in some seasons, particularly if there has been a lot of sunshine.

Soils

Some soils are capable of giving good colours, particularly those with a high iron content. As many pigments for paint are manufactured from earths it is always worth experimenting with your garden soil to see if it will produce colour. The red soils of Devon and Somerset and those of brick-earth areas together with Pennine peats all give useful colours on wool.

Ancient Dyes 8

If man was indeed using colour as early as 20,000 years ago to create the cave paintings of Lascaux and Altamira, we are forced to admit that he was civilized to a degree unrealized before their discovery. We shall never know the full extent of his early efforts at dyeing with plants, insects and earth pigments and can only guess at the spread of knowledge and techniques. Tiny fragments of coloured cloth have been unearthed at many sites of early civilization and it is reasonable to assume that skills were mainly spread by diffusion rather than by spontaneous inspiration although this too seems to have occurred at some periods of history.

Gradually, as the art of dyeing developed, the use of coloured cloth became universal among all classes of society, whereas formerly only the ruling classes, kings, army commanders and priests had been privileged to wear certain colours. The Greeks prized the saffron plant for its yellow dye; the Phoenicians produced purple from several related species of shellfish; blue from indigo was used in China for silk and cotton clothing; and in India, red from lac and madder and brown from cutch was used to dye cotton. We have inherited much from the traditions of early dyers and many of the plants and insects which they used are still obtainable today; others, however, like the shellfish which produced crimson and purple dye, are all but obsolete or have been replaced by more economical sources. It would be a pity to ignore the experience of any craftsman in any age, however remote, and no manual would be complete without some reference to the materials which dyers of the past used so successfully, for ancient textiles have retained their colours to a remarkable degree: a sure sign of the skill of their creators.

Sadly, few of our ancestors were interested in recording the details of the dye industry, nor had they museums where tools or obsolete materials could be stored as a record of their industrial past. As knowledge increased and better sources of colour were discovered, one dye plant after another was discarded and the old methods of preparation were often lost. For example, at one stage in the Middle Ages woad and madder were plants of such importance that whole economies in Western Europe revolved round their culture and use, but when indigo and cochineal were imported into Europe they were superseded and eventually declined almost to extinction.

The lack of records proved a considerable hindrance to me when I began to experiment with woad, for I found it well nigh impossible to track down a reliable recipe for using the fresh leaves, apart from the large-scale method in use on the Fenland farms in which much of the blue colour was lost by balling and drying. For the Fenland farmer this did not matter as his product was only used in recent times as a ferment for the indigo vats. In my search for a way of conserving the blue I had to evolve my own methods by trial and error, and in the early stages it seemed to be chiefly error.

The most ancient dyes used by man fall into three groups:

1. Dyes from shellfish, which gave greens, blues, crimson and purple.
2. Insect dyes. These included colours from a related group of insects called the *Coccidae*, which produced kermes and St John's blood in Europe,

lac in India and the Far East, and cochineal in North and South America.

3. Those from plants, which included blue from indigo and woad and several other indican-producing species (see Chapter 9); yellow from weld; red from madder and other related species.

Shellfish Dye: Tyrian Purple

Before 1500 BC the Phoenicians built a dye industry at Sidon and its offshoot colony Tyre. Great navigators and traders, scouring the coasts of Western Europe for supplies of tin for their bronze smelting, they also established dye works at sites where murex and buccinium shellfish had been discovered. Both types of sea snail are voracious carnivores and will bore holes with their toothed tongue-ribbons through the shells of other molluscs, but they will also eat dead meat and they can be trapped in creel-like pots. This famous pair, like the common dog whelk (*Nucella lapillus*), yield a drop or two of colourless fluid from the hypobranchial gland after the outer shells of the spines have been broken off. The liquid, which is also present in the eggs of the dog whelk, changes on exposure to air from yellow to green, then blue, purple and red. The indians of Ecuador and Mexico have been reported to milk the juice from living molluscs by gentle squeezing.

Extracting the purple dye in ancient times was laborious and evil-smelling work and only the very high price obtained for the dyed cloth justified the cost of the huge labour force required. Divers have reported that the smell of Tyrian purple dye was like garlic and *Assa foetida* mixed together – a truly fearsome combination!

Formerly the word 'purple' covered a much wider range of colour than we understand by it today, accustomed as we are to the aniline dye first made by William Henry Perkins in 1856. Purple could mean anything from rose, red, heliotrope, crimson, sea green or blue to violet or almost black. All of these shades were regulated by the boiling and dyeing process and required great skill in management.

For two thousand years Tyrian purple was one of the three most precious dyes, but after 1453 and the fall of Constantinople it was no longer available to Christendom and in 1464 Pope Paul I was obliged to accept robes dyed with Polish cochineal for his cardinals. The great era of the shellfish industry ground to a halt and has never been revived: in modern terms the equivalent would probably be the closure of all the ICI factories. Today all that remains of the early dye-factory sites are vast mounds composed of millions of shells – thousands of shells were necessary to produce just 1oz of dye.

Why was Tyrian purple abandoned? Did the supply of molluscs run out from over-use? Many questions remain unanswered for the historians of the future. One can only regret that some tiny pocket of resistance did not survive so that we could see for ourselves the fast and beautiful colours derived from so humble a source of simple shellfish.

Insect Dyes

KERMES

Of the four related insect dyes, cochineal, lac, St John's blood and kermes, the last named is considered to be the oldest and most durable. Many ancient European tapestries are dyed with kermes, alum being the mordant in most general use with it in early times. Copper and iron were also employed and ammonia from stale urine was used as a colour modifier.

Kermes is made from the small dried bodies of the female shield louse (*Coccus ilicis*), which lives on the leaves of the kermes oak (*Quercus coccifera*), a

These colours achieved with natural dyes are unmatched by those which are chemically produced. (Ray Harwood.)

low shrub of upwards of 12ft in height with evergreen leaves like holly, and the holm oak (*Quercus ilex*), found along the coasts of the Mediterranean Sea and inland from the coasts of Greece. The females of the *Coccus* species attach themselves to the host plant by their mouths and spend their lives sucking plant juices and increasing rapidly in size. The first step in the dye-making process is the collection of these insects for drying in the sun and pickling in vinegar as a preservative until they are required.

Kermes is the Arabic name for *Coccus ilicis*; Latin scholars referred to it as *Grana tinctorium*, for ancient dyers believed the insect emerged from a grain or berry and referred to wool dyed with kermes as 'dyed in the grain'. First recorded in 1727 BC, kermes was used for dyeing wool, silk and leather and the colours were considered to be brighter than those from madder and faster than those from cochineal.

In this country kermes is extremely difficult to obtain at the present time, no doubt because the cost of gathering and drying the insects has outweighed the demand, particularly since the advent of aniline dyes in the last years of the nineteenth century. It would be worth looking for supplies if one visited any of the Mediterranean countries for a holiday, even if this entailed gathering the insects for oneself and storing them in vinegar until they could be used at a later date.

All the insect dyes may be treated in the same manner, using the same quantities of mordant as for cochineal, but bearing in mind that the old dyers regarded kermes as weaker than cochineal, so that in recipes using 4oz of cochineal per 1lb of wool the quantity of kermes should be doubled to 8oz. Unlike woad, kermes has an aromatic smell and is pleasant to use.

To Use Kermes for Dyeing
1. Wash and rinse the wool.
2. Mordant the wool with either alum, chrome, stannous chloride or copper.
3. Soak the kermes (allowing 8oz per 1lb of wool) overnight and then simmer gently for one and a half hours.
4. Strain off the liquid and use as the dyebath, adding 1 cupful of vinegar.
5. Simmer the kermes again and extract all the colour, using the solution to obtain paler shades.

ST JOHN'S BLOOD

One of the most interesting insect dyes of medieval times, St John's Blood, was confined to Eastern Europe where the host plant German knotgrass (*Scleranthus perennis*) flourished on the sandy wastes in Poland (hence the insect's name *Margarodes polonicus*), Lithuania and parts of Russia. The red dye was obtained by uprooting the host plant and harvesting the insects, which are similar to kermes and cochineal, from the roots. The plant was then replanted, not always successfully.

For a short period the host plants were cultivated specially for the provision of dye, and many monasteries imposed a tithe on the land where the insects were harvested. Bancroft records that the females, having been impregnated by the males, enlarged and prepared to bring forth their young about the time of the summer solstice, on St John's eve. At this time they contained a crimson juice which was used by the Turks and Armenians for dyeing wool, silk and animal hair. Like many another dye source, St John's blood suffered an eclipse when a better and cheaper red dye was discovered in Central America.

COCHINEAL

Europeans had for centuries relied on kermes and madder as sources of red dye so that there was considerable interest in 1518 when the Spaniards entered Mexico and discovered the indians dyeing their textiles red with cochineal, a dyestuff made from the dried bodies of the insect *Dactylopius coccus*. The natives used small brushes for harvesting the insects as the *Opuntia* cactus on which they live is extremely prickly. This method is still used for harvesting the insects.

Like silkworms, which will survive on oak, hawthorn or lettuce as well as on mulberry leaves, the *Coccidae* may be found on more than one type of host plant, and the dye from their bodies will vary with their food, as the quality of silk varies with the food of the silkworm.

Dyers argue endlessly about the colours they expect from natural sources but one must always expect variations – mainly due to soil and climatic differences – when dealing with unique material. It is far more important for the dyer to develop an instinctive feeling for colours, which comes from making many experiments, than to follow dye recipes slavishly. Quantities of dyestuff too are only to be used as a rough guide, for each year's products will vary according to the amount of sunshine and rainfall. Books should also be used chiefly for guidance and stimulus. I have only to read that it is impossible to obtain such and such a colour from a plant for me to get out my dyepot and make a test to see whether the statement is true. So often it is not. The writer may not have been sufficiently curious or patient to try out a full range of mordants, or to substitute fermentation if simmering failed to produce a result.

Today there is renewed interest in Cochineal among dyers in America, and it is gathered from a wide variety of cactus species including the *Opuntia*. The invading Spaniards found that cochineal cultivation was limited to the host plants of a few cactus species, particularly the thorny *Opuntia* and the smooth *Nopalea cochinellifera* found in the Oaxaca region of Mexico. Following its discovery, the crop proved so lucrative and in such demand in Europe that cochineal became part of the tribute paid to the crown of Spain in the middle of the sixteenth century. Although the cost of cochineal was high it compared favourably with kermes, for it gave a stronger dye and far less of it was required.

At first dyers resisted the use of cochineal, but eventually it replaced kermes as the principal red insect dye. It was inevitable that cochineal cultivation, once discovered, should be attempted outside its country of origin. In the days of long sea voyages enterprising travellers and seamen copied the Mexican indians and used the succulent *Opuntia* cactus as shipboard food, planting any surplus when they arrived at their destinations. The fleshy pads of the *Opuntia* strike readily and flourish in a variety of soils. In this way the host plant of *Dactylopius coccus* came to be translated from its native Mexico to every warm country in the world. Today it is to be found in Australia, South Africa, North and South America and in the Far East. The limiting factors appear to be temperature and length of daylight. Besides being a valuable and beautiful dyestuff for textiles, cochineal is still used as a food colorant and it may have an assured future as so many manufactured food dyes are now suspected of being carcinogenic.

The colouring principle of cochineal, carminic acid, produces beautiful crimsons, scarlets and pinks on wool and silk when mordanted with alum or tin with the addition of cream of tartar. With chrome, copper or iron mordants the colours range from purples to greys. The brightest colours of all come from a combination of tin and an acid, such as distilled vinegar, lemon juice, oxalic or tannic acid. Both Bancroft and Hellot state that 1oz of cochineal is sufficient to dye 1lb of wool. Modern recipes usually quote larger quantities, as much as 8oz per 1lb for very dark colours. Much depends on the quality and the strength of each batch of insects, and variations are considerable.

It is interesting to note that the host plants of both kermes and cochineal also give good colours. The leaves of the two kermes oaks yield warm rosy tans when they are soaked and simmered without mordants, and the *Opuntia polycantha* cactus, one of three hundred-odd species found in North and South America, gives reds and pinks on fermentation. The cactus is fermented in water in a non-metallic container for about two weeks; then the wool is entered and left for a similar time. No heat is needed apart from warmth from the sun, for like the colours from madder too much heat turns the red to orange or yellow tans.

To Dye with Cochineal

1. Quick all-in-one method.

½ lb unmordanted wool
2 oz alum
¾ oz cream of tartar
¾ oz cochineal

Dissolve the alum and cream of tartar in warm soft water and add it to 8 pints of tepid rainwater. Add the clean wet wool and simmer for twenty minutes. Take out the wool and add the cochineal, stirring until it is well dissolved. Re-enter the wool and simmer again for an hour, or longer for deep shades. Cool the wool in the dye liquid and then rinse. Use the dyebath again until all the colour is exhausted.

2. Using premordanted wool.

Below is a list of the colours which can be obtained with the various mordants:

Alum and cream of tartar: dark red
Tin and cream of tartar: scarlet
Iron: slate blue to black
Oxalic acid: rose to geranium red
Bichromate of potash: deep plum-purple

For deep rich colours allow 8 oz cochineal for 1 lb of wool; for softer colours allow 4 oz per 1 lb. Mix the cochineal, which looks like small dried pellets, to a paste with warm water. As the mixture will swell, allow plenty of room in the bowl or saucepan. Add the cochineal to 2–3 gals of warm water and stir well to smooth out any lumps. Bring to simmering point and hold for ten minutes, then cool to hand heat. Have ready the damp wool or silk, previously mordanted. Add this to the dyebath and simmer gently for an hour. Cool the wool or silk in the dyebath until quite cold, then squeeze gently and rinse until the water is clear. Shake out the moisture and dry in the shade. Use the dyebath again until all the colour is exhausted. You will be surprised at the amount of colour which can be extracted from one cochineal bath, and at the strength of the colours.

LAC

The lac insect (*Lakshadia chinensis; Lakshadia communis*) is a parasite on over eighty plant species, but of this number only seven are of economic importance. These are: *Acacia arabica, Cajanus cajan, Ficus religiosa, Zizzyphus xylopyrus, Zizzyphus jujuba, Butea monosperma* and *Schleichera oleoda*. The insects are found wild in Tibet and China as well as in Burma, Siam and India. The word *lac* in Hindu means 'one hundred thousand', and is usually applied to rupees, but it aptly describes the insects when they are swarming on the host plants.

Lac dye has been used for many centuries in both the old world and the new. William Partridge, the American dyer, writing in 1823, gives a complicated process for dyeing scarlet, using cream of tartar, lac lake, turmeric, safflower, cochineal and oil of vitriol. On reading through this recipe one is reminded of the eighteen processes which were used for the manufacture of Turkey red from madder. However, fine scarlets were also produced more simply from lac with tin as the mordant, and carmine colours with alum.

To make the dye the insects are collected off the twigs of the host plant, broken up and added to hot water, or a solution of sodium carbonate, to remove the dye matter, laccaic acid. With lime or alum the acid is precipitated as lac dye. There are many mineral and resinous impurities in lac dye and it yields its colour to water less readily than cochineal. Twelve hours before it is to be used as a

A woven stole and two hooked rugs made with naturally dyed wool. (Ray Harwood.)

CUTCH

Cutch or catechu (*Acacia catechu*; *Aria catechu*) is a very ancient brown dye much used in India for cottons. Prepared from the wood of certain acacia trees, it comes on to the market in the shape of dark brown cubes which require pounding well before they are used. To make these the wood is processed as follows: the trees are felled and the outside of the logs is removed; the inner wood is made into chips which are then boiled, the liquid is evaporated and the resulting thick sludge is spread out in the hot sunshine to dry, after which it is divided into cubes like chocolate.

Cutch will dye wool, silk and cotton a yellowish brown. With iron, it gives grey-browns, and with copper, olive tones. Dyeing usually takes place before mordanting.

In India cutch was once also much used for tanning leather, a useful point for sheep breeders who cure and tan their own sheepskins.

To Dye with Cutch

Dissolve the cutch in soft water. Add the wet wool or cotton. Simmer until the desired depth of colour is obtained. Old recipes allow 10 to 20 per cent cutch to each dyebath. As the strength varies with the age of each batch it is best to experiment with a tiny quantity first.

FUSTIC

Fustic for dyeing is prepared from the dyer's mulberry tree (*Morus tinctoria* or *Chlorophora tinctoria*) which is indigenous to the West Indies and Mexico and is known as Cuba fustic. The wood is a sulphur yellow and the dye from it is substantive. If mordants are used the colours are extremely fast.

Fustic is very useful for making Saxon greens in combination with woad or indigo and it is a very useful dye substance for mixing with many other colours. Below is a list of colours which are obtainable with various mordants and other dyestuffs:

Bichromate of potash: old gold
Stannous chloride and cream of tartar: bright yellow
Logwood and bichromate of potash: greenish yellow
Woad or Indigo: bright greens
Copper sulphate: olive green
Ferrous sulphate: dark greens

As with logwood, each batch of dye material will vary in strength so that it is best to simmer a small weighed quantity of wool and dyestuff before embarking on large batches.

QUERCITRON

Two species of oak, *Quercus nigra* and *Quercus tinctoria*, growing in the United States and Central America yield a brilliant yellow dye from their inner bark. Edward Bancroft is reputed to have introduced quercitron into England in 1785 as a substitute for weld. Flavine is an extract of quercitron bark and the dye may be bought in either bark or liquid form.

If in bark form the dye material should be soaked in soft water at 100°F and then simmered for an hour or two. Alkalis will deepen the colours and acids will brighten them. The following colours may be obtained with the appropriate mordants and/or dyestuffs:

Alum and cream of tartar: yellows
Cochineal on alum mordanted wool: orange
Indigo: green colours

TURMERIC

Turmeric is a yellow powder made from the ground-up tubers of *Curcuma longa* or *Curcuma tinctoria*, plants which grow in India, Java, China and Madagascar. The dye is substantive and is one of the first to be chosen by novice dyers as it is

Splendid hooked and crocheted rugs illustrate some different effects which can be achieved with plant dyes. (Ray Harwood.)

easily obtainable as a food colouring in grocers' shops and is relatively cheap.

Turmeric has the reputation of being a fugitive dye and prone to fade, so I always plunge my dyed wool into a strong solution of Maldon salt and water to set the dye and this seems to work well. An alternative would be to rinse the wool in salt sea water as is done in Palestine.

To Dye with Turmeric
Dissolve 2 teaspoonfuls of turmeric powder in 6 pints of soft water, together with a pinch of stannous chloride, and stir well. Enter the clean wet wool and slowly bring to simmering point, holding for fifteen minutes. Leave the wool to cool in the dye saucepan. Rinse. Wash and rinse again. Soak in salt water and dry.

SAFFRON

Originally cultivated in the Middle East, particularly in Persia, Kurdistan, Greece and Asia Minor, saffron (*Crocus sativus*) was imported into England many centuries ago and was once grown in great quantities at Saffron Walden in Essex. The dye is made from the three long bright orange stigmas of the crocus flowers and it has been computed that 60,000 stigmas will make 1lb of saffron dye. With so many other yellow dye sources available to us today saffron is therefore unlikely to ever be revived as a crop, but a small dyebath may be made experimentally for the interest of using such an historic dye plant.

To Dye with Saffron
Gently simmer 1 teaspoonful of dried saffron in a cupful of soft water. Enter a small tuft of clean, wet wool and simmer for thirty minutes. Cool in the dye liquid. Rinse. Dry in the shade.

SUMACH

There are several varieties of the *Rhus* species which yield useful colours ranging from yellow to brown red, depending on whether the leaves, seeds or berries are used. Sumach thrives in the temperate parts of Europe (*Rhus coriara*), Asia and America (*Rhus glabra*) and has been used not only as a dye plant for wool but also for tanning leather, the roots and stem being employed for this purpose. It was a very important dye for the American colonists and was also much used by the indians of North America. Sumach contains tannic and gallic acid, enabling it to be used as a substantive dye, though alum is often used as a mordant for making rich tan colours from the berries.

The leaves, roots, shoots and bark all give dye. The berries are collected ripe before the first frosts; the leaves and stalks in late summer when fully mature.

There are several toxic members of the *Rhus* family which should *not* be used for dyeing, particularly *Rhus vernix* and *Rhus radicans*. Both have white and not red berries and are therefore easily distinguished as being unsafe to use.

To Dye with Sumach
Soak 1lb of ripe sumach berries for two days in cold soft water. Heat to simmering point and simmer slowly for three hours. Strain off the berries and allow the liquor to become cold. Enter clean wet wool and raise the dyebath to simmering point. Hold for fifteen minutes and remove from the heat. Allow the wool to cool in the dyebath. Rinse and dry the wool.

HENNA

Henna is an excellent substantive dye made from Egyptian privet (*Lawsonia inermis*) which has been used for centuries as a beauty aid for the hair and finger nails. As well as Egypt, the shrub is also indigenous to India, Persia and Palestine. The dye is made from the dried leaves, which are picked, dried and made into a paste or powder containing hennotannic acid.

To Dye with Henna

> 4oz wool or silk
> 4oz henna
> a pinch of stannous chloride

Dissolve the henna in warm soft water. Dissolve the tin and add to the henna bath and stir well. Enter the clean wet wool and simmer slowly for one hour. Cool the wool in the dye liquor. Rinse. Wash and rinse again.

WELD

Weld (*Reseda luteola*), also called wild mignonette and dyer's greenweed, is probably older than any other yellow dye and has been used for many centuries to give brilliant, fast colours on both wool and silk. When used on cotton, it is not fast to soap. In the Middle Ages it was used with dyer's broom (*Genista tinctoria*) for making Kendal green and Lincoln green.

Weld is extremely easy to grow as it will flourish on the poorest soil, springing up on waste places, old tips, the edges of chalk pits, building sites and where the subsoil is chalk or limestone. Native throughout the Mediterranean region and indigenous to England, weld was cultivated as a dye crop a century ago in Kent, Herefordshire and in the Doncaster area, as well as in France, Germany and Italy. In medieval times much weld was imported from Normandy. Today dyers value this plant for the brilliance of the colours, which may be obtained by using a wide range of mordants.

In the wild state weld grows as a biennial. The plants seed in September and small bright green rosettes appear and winter hardily before shooting into flowering stems the following summer. If weld is deliberately cultivated as a dye plant it may be sown in the garden in February and March in drills, or broadcast at the rate of 8 pints of seed per acre on a field scale. The plants should be thinned to 6 ins. apart in each direction. Weld is pulled for dyeing in mid- to late July, and some of the plants are left for seed. The whole plant above ground may be chopped and simmered fresh, or carefully dried for use during the winter. There is little difference in the depth of yellow colour from fresh or dried plants but the range of greens is greater from freshly cut leaves and stems.

I first grew weld for dyeing when I moved into Essex in 1945 and found a small plantation of it growing by the river winding through the farm. A few August-sown seeds ensured a continuing crop for thirty years, for the plants seeded themselves in every corner of the garden. If I had room for only three dye plants in my garden weld would be one of them, for it is hardy, easy to grow and produces a large amount of dyestuff in concentrated form from a small area of ground. It is one of the most useful dyes for making greens on its own or with woad or indigo.

Weld grows up to 3ft in height before flowering, the stems are hollow and furrowed and the long flower spikes resemble mignonette, but they have no scent until they are simmered for dyeing when they produce a strong asparagus-like smell.

To Dye with Weld

I find that 1lb weld to 1lb of wool provides adequate colours, but double the amount of weld to wool will give outstanding greens. Salt seems to enrich and deepen the colours and the dyers of former times always added 1oz of powdered chalk to 1lb of weld.

Chop and cover the weld with soft water and simmer gently for one and a half hours. Strain off the juice and use it as the dyebath. Enter the premordanted wool and simmer gently for another one and a half hours.

The following colours can be obtained from weld:

Alum and cream of tartar: bright acid yellows
Stannous chloride and cream of tartar: daffodil yellow

*Weld (*Reseda luteola*) in full flower. (Enid Tivey.)*

Bichromate of potash: gold
Ferrous sulphate and cream of tartar: moss green
Copper sulphate and cream of tartar: soft yellow
Copper sulphate, cream of tartar and Stannous chloride: brilliant green
Copper sulphate, cream of tartar and ammonia: very fine, deep moss green
Copper sulphate and cream of tartar with Ferrous sulphate added for the last fifteen minutes of the dyebath: bronze and olive greens.

Weld is one of the plants which may be used as a 'simultaneous' dye – that is, one for which the mordant is dissolved in hot water and added to the dyebath after the plant material has been strained off. The colours are just as fast and as deep as those obtained by the usual method of mordanting the fibre before dyeing.

MADDER

*A flourishing group of madder plants (*Rubia tinctoria*) in full leaf. (Enid Tivey.)*

Now that kermes and cochineal are both scarce and expensive, madder (*Rubia tinctoria*) is becoming ever more important to dyers in large temperate areas of the world where it may easily be grown as a good source of red dye material. Known as a dye plant for centuries and mentioned in the writings of Pliny the Elder as growing near Rome in the first century AD, madder was taken to Spain by the Arabs and spread through to Minorca and Italy.

The genus *Rubia* occurs in many countries, from North and South America to large tracts of Asia and Europe. In the British Isles are found several members of the family which all yield good red dyes from their woody roots: Lady's bedstraw (*Galium verum*), hedge bedstraw (*Galium mollugo*), northern bedstraw (*Galium boreale*), dyer's woodruff (*Galium odoratum*) and goosegrass or cleavers (*Galium aparine*). The propagation of these plants is identical with that of madder, but it must be remembered that they are smaller and finer and more of them will be required to achieve a deep colour. Madder roots are unmistakable because of their size and earthy red colour, but the roots of cleavers, woodruff and the bedstraws (all of which may be grown in plots like madder) are not so easily distinguished when dug. Many people never find the dyeing root at all as they think that the fine roots attached to the plant base are the ones used, whereas it is the thicker woody roots well below the surface which yield the dye.

The red dye in madder is present in the root in the form of glucosides, the most important of which is ruberthyric acid which is made up of sugar and the dyeing agent alizarin. The roots also contain rubian, tannin and purpurin. The alizarin occurs as orange or red crystals in the root cells, almost insoluble in water but soluble in alcohol or alkaline solutions. The dye from madder has been used in experiments with the growth of bones and will also colour milk and urine if fed to animals.

We know from old records and writings that the deepest colour obtainable from madder comes from plants which are grown in soil containing a high proportion of chalk or lime, and it is worth noting at this point that madder and other plants of the same genus will give better colours if the dyebath is made with *hard* water. In soft water districts, therefore, add a little slaked lime (calcium hydroxide) or some ground chalk to each dyebath.

Madder growers in medieval Europe evolved elaborate systems of harvesting and crushing the roots of what at that time was an extremely valuable crop. As well as large crushing mills they had drying houses and tubs for storage. In eastern countries, to avoid the risk of adulteration, the whole roots of the plant were dried in the open air and sold to the dyers as they were. Old records state that the soil must be rested for ten years between each crop of madder to avoid exhaustion. The Dutch growers only allowed the plant to remain in the ground for two years lest the roots should undermine their elaborate field-drainage and dyke systems.

Ancient Hebrew laws permitted the growing of madder for domestic but not commercial use, and stated that only wooden tools were to be used for harvesting. One wonders what practical or religious reason lay at the root of this decree, so like the rule which bound the Druids to using a golden sickle for harvesting mistletoe.

The famous Turkey red was obtained from madder root by first separating its two distinct colours, fawn and red, and using the latter, in much the same way as the colour from safflower is divided into red and yellow by washing. Suitable for either wool or cotton, the dye was produced by long and complicated processes requiring the use of sumach and oak galls, calf's blood, sheep's dung, oil, soda, alum and a solution of tin. Levantine dyers were reluctant to disclose the method by which these substances were used and for long the process remained a closely guarded secret.

From prehistoric times until the middle of the nineteenth century madder was a dye of supreme commercial importance, as supplies could be increased or decreased according to demand and laws regulating its growth existed in most European countries. When in 1869 Graebe and Liebermann produced synthetic alizarin in the laboratory, the disastrous collapse of the madder industry was inevitable, as occurred with indigo a little later. Eventually large areas went out of cultivation in Holland and France where madder had been used for dyeing the cloth of army uniforms. In Great Britain madder continued to be used in the production of hunting pink for high-quality cloth for hunting coats.

Cultivation, Harvesting and Storage
The root of madder is perennial, with an annual

stalk. It is very deep-growing and will spread rapidly in good clean soil. From the roots spring large, square, jointed stalks which will grow to a height of several feet and need staking. The flowers are small and yellow and appear only in the second or third year, in June; the seeds look like small black peppercorns.

Madder growers in England leave the plants undisturbed, apart from cultivations, for three to five years. They are then dug in August when the thick reddish roots are lifted, sorted and dried carefully after cleaning, and the root stalks are replanted in fresh ground. It is best to divide up the area in which madder is to be grown into four sections and to plant and dig up one section each year in rotation, thus ensuring a continuous supply of roots. Personally I find that the best plants grow from two-year-old shoots divided from the parent plant and set out in May, when the apple trees are in bloom. Watering is essential after planting, until the new shoots are obviously thriving in their new situation.

After lifting, madder roots should be washed and scrubbed to remove all the loose soil. If they are dug after a week or two of fine weather they will be easier to clean. An old picture frame covered in cotton sheeting makes a good drying rack: spread the roots out evenly over the surface and keep in a warm place until they are crisp and dry. Alternatively, place them on wire-mesh cake racks inside a cool oven. Once dried, the roots will store for a long period without deterioration in glass or earthenware jars or paper bags, either whole or ground into a powder.

To Dye with Fresh Home-grown or Bought Madder
In the case of home-grown madder, dig, clean and dry the roots. As the dye is chiefly between the woody centre of the root and the outer skin, use the whole root. Allowing 3oz of fresh madder roots or ½oz (10 teaspoonfuls) of commercial madder to each gallon of *hard* water, soak overnight with 2 teaspoonfuls of powdered chalk added.

As in dyeing with woad and indigo, the temperature of the dyebath is crucial: a thermometer must be used as much colour will be lost if the dyebath exceeds 158°F. Raise the temperature from cold to 158°F within an hour, never allowing the liquid to exceed simmering point. The best colours are obtained at 140°F; above this the shades change from reds to browns. Strain off the madder roots and use the liquor as the dyebath. Re-simmer the roots with more hard water and use for paler shades. Enter clean wet mordanted wool and continue simmering for thirty to forty minutes. Allow the fibres to cool in the dyebath, rinse them thoroughly when cold, wash in warm soapy water, rinse again and dry in the open air.

The following colours are obtainable with various mordants:

Alum and cream of tartar: red
Stannous chloride and cream of tartar: bright orange
Bichromate of potash: red, orange
Bichromate of potash with ½ teaspoonful of ferrous sulphate added for the last fifteen minutes of simmering: deep, dark red

Indigo 9

Indigo, which has been known as 'the king of dyestuffs' for many centuries, is one of the oldest-known dyes. It continues to be of great economic importance, for so few plants yield fast blue colours that it far outshines all its rivals. For over five thousand years indigo from plants has been used to dye wool, silk, cotton and other natural fibres, but in 1887 a German chemist, Adolf von Baeyer, discovered a method of synthesizing the first artificial indigo in the laboratory. From that time to the present day the production of natural plant indigo has steadily declined and the range of plants from which it is derived have been cultivated less and less for the world markets and more for local consumption. Without von Baeyer's discovery and the subsequent development of synthetic indigo there would not have been the world-wide explosion of blue denim clothing which we have experienced in the decades since the Second World War, for the old system of producing plant indigo would never have kept pace with the demand for it.

The modern dyer will have increasing difficulty in obtaining supplies of natural plant indigo unless he grows his own, and he must sometimes be prepared to accept the very pure and concentrated manufactured blue powder which is offered by the dye houses for what it is — a good substitute for the natural product, but not to my mind as beautiful in use. Both kinds of indigo are chemically the same substance, but the synthetic indigo contains no plant residues or other remains which are responsible for many subtle variations in shade, so that much less of it is required to dye a given quantity of fibre. A quarter of the amount given in recipes using natural indigo is quite sufficient.

Indigo is a dark blue crystalline powder which is insoluble in water, ether or alcohol, but soluble in nitrobenzene, chloroform or concentrated sulphuric acid, none of which are substances a dyer would care to use on precious handspun yarns without great caution. The chemical formula for indigo is $C_{16} H_{10} N_2 O_2$ and in the laboratory it is manufactured with aniline, which by reaction with formaldehyde and sodium cyanide yields phenylglycene. The latter, on fusion with a mixture of sodomide and caustic potash, is changed to indoxyl, the oxidation of which leads to indigo.

In the leaves of indigo-bearing plants the naturally occurring precursor of indigo is indican, a colourless water-soluble substance that is easily hydrolysed to glucose and indoxyl. The latter is converted to indigo by mild oxidation, i.e. exposure to air. The use of plant species containing the glucoside indican is extremely ancient and occurs far back in the remote past. We do not know whether these species were discovered at roughly the same time or at widely different intervals in man's history, but the finding of the first blue-dye-bearing plant may have stimulated a search for others and even at this late date it is just possible that some still remain to be discovered. As both blue and red dyes are few and far between, any reliable source of these plants is of immense economic importance, particularly if they can be renewed by cultivation.

At the present time the species of plants which are known to contain indigo are: the indigoferas; woad, a crucifer; *Polygonum tinctorium*, a dye-bearing polygonum similar to *Polygonum persicaria*; *Nerium tinctorium*, an indican-bearing oleander; Marsdenia; and *Lonchocarpus cyanescens*. Of these the first two named have always been the most important but the others are also of interest should any reader travel to Sumatra, West Africa, or to India.

All natural dye material must be dissolved in a liquid before fibres can absorb the colours, but there are problems with indigo which occur with no other dye plants and to come to grips with them a little knowledge of plant chemistry is necessary. In all the indigo-bearing plants indigo is present as a colourless glucoside which will not change into a blue insoluble compound until it has combined with atmospheric oxygen. J. J. Hummel in *The Dyeing of Textile Fibres* (1896) puts it in a nutshell: 'The method *par excellence* in dyeing with indigo is founded on the property it possesses of being converted under the influence of reducing agents, i.e. bodies capable of yielding nascent hydrogen, into indigo white, which is soluble in alkaline solutions.' The formula for this chemical change is as follows:

Indigotin = $C_{16}H_{10}N_2O_2 + H_2 =$
 $C_{16}H_{12}N_2O_2$ = indigo white

on oxidation this gives $C_{16}H_{10}N_2O_2$ = indigo

A few folk tales exist in primitive cultures about the way in which reducing agents were first discovered but we know very little historically of the hit-and-miss methods which were used first and which gradually evolved into the more complicated procedures of modern times. Undoubtedly early dyers worked empirically without fully realizing the steps involved in the reduction of indican to indigo white; indeed accident and coincidence must account for many of man's most important discoveries. As a woad grower I can easily see how woad developed as an important source of indigo, for when the first-year leaves are picked the yellow sticky juice soon turns blue on the hands and will take several days to fade or wash away. The burning question for the earliest dyers would have been how to transfer this splendid colour to wool, silk or cotton after seeing it on their hands. It is possible that when the two simplest ferments, stale urine and wood ash, were used successfully with one species of indigo-bearing plant they may have been tried with other groups, including woad.

The stages of indigo production and dyeing from all the known plant species containing indican are as follows.

STAGE 1: EXTRACTION OF THE DYE

(a) The plant leaves are picked when fully developed.
(b) The leaves are torn, minced or chopped to release the plant juice.
(c) The mass of plant pulp is either used at once for a fresh dyebath, *or* if the dye is to be stored for some time the pulp is made up into large balls and carefully dried, being compressed by hand as they shrink. Drying for storage is wasteful with woad, however, as much of the blue is lost — it is far better to make the woad into a solution, add an alkali after beating the liquid and then store the solution with sodium metabisulphite as a preservative.

STAGE 2: DYEING

(a) The indican in the balls or solution must now be converted to indigo white with a reducing agent.
(b) After reduction the indigo white is dissolved in an alkali.
(c) The clean wet fibres are dipped in the dissolved indigo white and then aired. This causes the dye to re-oxidise on the fibres, making a very fast and permanent blue dye.

A properly made indigo bath made with synthetic indigo should be clear yellow in colour and the dipped fibres from it will emerge yellow and slowly turn yellow-green, green, green-blue and then blue after exposure to air. The longer the fibres are allowed to soak in the clear yellow solution, the deeper will be the colour when they emerge. They should be dipped and aired for the same length of time. Five minutes dipped and five airing will give pale to mid-blues, an hour's soaking and airing will result in deep blues and navy blues, and blue-blacks may be attained with still longer immersion and airing.

The process for using laboratory-made indigo is exactly the same as for the natural plant product. The powder is reduced to indigo white, dissolved in an alkali and the fibres are then dyed. The colours will be much more uniform than those achieved with natural indigo because there are no plant residues, though, as already stated, they will not necessarily be more acceptable to dyers.

When dyeing with fresh plant indigo one must not expect a clear yellow dyebath on reduction: the colour is more likely to be dark green. If, however, the plant matter (with the exception of woad) has been dried before use the clear yellow dyebath is more likely to be attained.

The perfect reducing agent for any of the indigo-bearing plants as well as for manufactured indigo is stale urine which has been stored in a closed airtight container for at least a fortnight to allow ammonia to develop. Not only is it plentiful and free, but it also leaves fibres, particularly wool, in far better condition than when alkalis such as caustic soda are used as a solvent. There may come a day when we have to rely entirely on natural products for our mordants and ferments and then urine will come into its own once again. It is still used extensively in many parts of the world and has never been abandoned by dyers of common sense with an eye to economy. The bacteria in urine require oxygen for survival which they obtain from urea, and in the course of their life cycle they liberate hydrogen which converts the indigo to indigo white. At this stage the ammonia in urea provides the necessary alkali for dissolving the indigo white, and after at least two weeks have been allowed for fermentation the yarn may be soaked in the solution and aired and permanent blue indigo will be deposited on the fibres. Dipping and airing should occupy the same length of time. Thorough soaking afterwards in plain soft water or with a mixture of sea salt and vinegar will rid the dyed yarns of any smell, after which they may be washed and rinsed several times until the rinsing water is clear.

The one drawback to using stale urine as the fermenting and reducing agent for indigo is the time factor. The urine must be kept for two to three weeks before adding the indigo, and another two weeks to allow the indigo to dissolve and reduce before dyeing can begin. The great advantages of the urine vat are its simplicity, cheapness and safety. No teacher, for instance, would care to use sulphuric acid as a solvent in a modern classroom as the risks would be too great, and few would take their chance with caustic soda. Both are extremely dangerous near the eyes.

When the use of the urine vat is inconvenient, however, there are several other safe alkalis and reducing agents which have been well tried and tested over the centuries. For dyeing wool, bulky materials like bran and madder will reduce indigo by fermentation to indigo white, and sodium carbonate will render it soluble for dyeing. Even wood-ash liquid makes a useful alkaline solution, while yeast, sugar and ammonia also prove effective, though only with natural indigo. The following mixtures have been used commercially on a large scale to dye cotton with indigo.

1. Bran, madder, chalk or quicklime (very fresh).
2. Ferrous sulphate, slaked lime.
3. Bran, treacle, carbonate of soda, slaked lime.
4. Zinc, slaked lime, water.

The Indigoferas

Over a century ago at least two dozen species of indigofera were known, all of them natives of tropical or semi-tropical climates, but not all of them dye-bearing. They are to be found in China, Java, the Malagasy Republic (formerly Madagascar), India, parts of southern Africa and in North and South America. The three species mainly cultivated for the production of blue dye are the East Indian *Indigofera tinctoria*, the West Indian *Indigofera anil* and the silver-leaved *Indigofera argentea*. Another species, *Indigofera suffruticosa*, which is very similar to *Indigofera tinctoria* but with smaller seed pods, is to be found in the southern states of North America.

Historians, anthropologists and botanists are still uncertain about the manner in which the various species of indigofera have spread with the growth of civilizations. Some assert that the Asian types were brought across the land bridge over what is now the Bering Straits more than 25,000 years ago. We do know that the use of indigo occurs in many ancient cultures but not whether knowledge was spread by diffusion – some historians lean to the theory that dyeing discoveries occurred roughly at the same time in different parts of the world. However and wherever they are found, indigo plants have been used for dyeing wool, silk and cotton.

Initially dyers processed comparatively small quantities of leaves and dyed with them in solution, reducing the indican to soluble indigo white with natural agents like stale urine, wood ash and bran. The Sumatrans still treat the leaves of their native marsdenia in this way, using wood ash only. As the demand for blue-dyed cloth increased over the centuries, however, a method of processing large quantities of leaves for storage and bulk use was evolved. In the case of woad, lonchocarpus and *Polygonum tinctorium* the leaves were carefully dried and compressed simultaneously. Polygonum and lonchocarpus balls dried quickly in the tropical climates where the plants occurred but woad took several weeks in a European summer and the balls were examined daily for cracks. If these appeared they were carefully closed by hand-squeezing as air had to be excluded from the fermenting centre. The balls were used for dyeing by first being broken and crushed before fermentation in an alkaline liquid.

The fermentation of the indigoferas was accomplished in a different manner. In the thirteenth century Marco Polo, one of the very first European travellers to India and China, noted the method of processing indigo in the kingdom of Coulan. He wrote: 'They procure it from an herbaceous plant, which is taken up by the roots, and put into tubs of water, where it is suffered to remain till it rots, when they press out the juice. This upon being exposed to the sun and evaporated leaves a kind of paste, which is cut into small pieces of the form in which we see it brought to us.' Marco Polo's admirably concise account omits three important points:

1. The indigofera was harvested when the leaves were at the peak of their growth, just before the plant flowered.
2. The plant matter was discarded after fermentation.
3. The indigotin solution was beaten with paddles to promote oxidation. When the oxidation was accomplished the indigo was allowed to settle as a blue sediment and the liquid was drawn off, allowing the sediment to dry so that it could be pressed and cut into blocks for the market. This was the dyestuff indigo.

In the entrance hall of the Plant Museum at Kew Gardens there is a model of an indigo factory which clearly shows all the stages of indigo production described above.

For many centuries indigo was sold in small blocks or as a blue powder and from the centres of

A model of an Indian indigo factory. (Crown copyright; reproduced with the permission of the Controller of Her Majesty's Stationery Office and of the Royal Botanic Gardens, Kew.)

production in the Middle and Far East it crept across continents by trading routes until it reached the Mediterranean countries and the areas where woad was used for the production of blue dye. Then battle was joined in earnest: no craftsman cares to abandon long-tried and successful processes. Europeans had built a vast industry on the cultivation, processing and use of woad and they were extremely reluctant to change to an unknown material. Inevitably those whose livelihood was threatened over-reacted. In Germany a decree of the Diet, held in 1577, prohibited under the severest penalties 'the newly invented, pernicious, deceitful, eating and corrosive dye called the Devil's Dye', for which vitriol and other eating substances were used instead of woad. The people of Normandy went further: their dyers were obliged to take an oath not to use indigo. However, in France, Colbert, who was far more enlightened and forward-looking had similar restrictions repealed in 1669 and from then on indigo superseded woad as the chief blue dye in the western hemisphere.

Today natural indigo is still obtainable in the countries where it is grown and processed but it is becoming increasingly difficult to buy as laboratory-made indigo is far more widely used. For three centuries in the West natural indigo reigned supreme, slowly and inexorably ousting woad from its pre-eminence. At first the dyers who used it were extremely cautious, suspecting it of evil qualities, indeed half-hoping for them, so that they could revert to their beloved native blue from woad. As it became obvious to them that indigo was both more economical and powerful as a dye they became bolder and began to experiment with it. However, woad was never completely abandoned in Britain until commercial production of it ceased in 1932 when the last woad farm in the Fens closed down.

Since the first introduction of indigo in Elizabethan times woad had been used with indigo as a natural ferment for it, albeit one not always easy to control, and many dyers affirmed that woaded cloths were of superior colour and fastness compared with those dyed solely with indigo – 'as blue as wad' is a very ancient dyer's simile. Then in the late nineteenth century a further development in the fermenting and reduction of indigo took place with the advent of sodium hydrosulphite. This was used with caustic soda, which acted as a potent alkali in dissolving the indigo white formed by the reduction of indican by the sodium hydrosulphite. Finally, when the vats were made with synthetic indigo in addition to these two substances, a once-natural dye process had been replaced entirely by chemicals.

CULTIVATION AND PROPAGATION

Though *Indigofera tinctoria* may be sown at all seasons in tropical climates, spring is the most usual time for sowing. The seeds should be planted in little furrows 4 ins. wide and 2–3 ins. in depth, 1ft apart. With plenty of moisture, germination is very rapid and can take as little as five days, and provided the plants are kept watered and weeded the crop is ready for cutting with a sickle in about eight weeks. Indigo plants grow up to 2ft in height, with winged leaves, and the tiny reddish flowers develop into small brown pods containing yellow seeds. Under warm conditions four crops of plant tops may be harvested in a year, but the amount diminishes with each cutting.

TO DYE WITH THE INDIGOFERAS

Three methods of using natural or manufactured indigo are:

1. *The Indigo Urine Vat*
Dissolve 2 teaspoonfuls of indigo powder by stirring into a gallon container of two-week-old urine. Leave the indigo to dissolve and ferment for a further two weeks keeping the container with the lid on in a warm place. The contents should be stirred daily. A temperature of 120°F speeds the fermentation. A hot airing cupboard or full sunshine out of doors are ideal, or place the container, pre-heated to the correct temperature, in a 'hay box' made from cardboard or wood and lined with old pillows, cushions, eiderdowns or even bags of sawdust. After two weeks the indigo will have broken down into soluble form. Immerse the clean wet fibre for dyeing and leave to soak for at least five days with the lid tightly closed. Again, warmth is necessary for the fermentation to continue. After five days air the wool or other fibres twice daily for thirty minutes at a time. When the desired depth of colour has been obtained, gently drain and squeeze the yarns and rinse in soft water containing 2 tablespoonfuls of vinegar and 1 tablespoonful of sea salt. Shake out in the air and wash in soft water and mild detergent or pure soap flakes. Rinse at least three times before drying and airing. Dry in the open air. Use the dyebath for further batches of wool until all the colour has been exhausted. The colours from successive baths will be paler but fast.

2. *The Indigo Soda Vat*
Pre-soak 1lb of wool or cotton in 1 gal of soft water containing 1 teaspoonful of well-dissolved washing soda. At the same time dissolve 6oz of washing soda in 8 pints of soft water. Add 2oz of indigo and whisk and stir for five minutes. Close the container with a tight-fitting lid and ferment at a temperature of about 90°F for four days, stirring well twice daily. To the indigo and soda vat add the pre-soaked wool or cotton and leave to soak for two days. Begin dipping and airing, allowing the fibre to remain an equal time in the air as in the liquid. Though greenish yellow in the liquid, the fibres turn blue in the air. Beautiful peacock blues may be obtained by this method but the temperature in the container should never exceed 125°F or much colour will be lost. If the fermentation is slow, a handful of bran may be added.

3. *The Indigo Hydrosulphite Vat*
Many recipes for this vat use caustic soda as the solvent. I have had one or two disasters using caustic soda and once completely dissolved some

hanks of precious hand-spun Shetland wool. All my notebooks bristle with injunctions such as 'Never use caustic soda, it ruins wool' clearly marked with asterisks. Washing soda is an adequate substitute, and this is used in the recipe given below:

   1oz indigo powder
   2oz washing soda
   4oz sodium hydrosulphite
   4 pints soft water

1. Add 8 fluid oz boiling soft water to the washing soda and stir until it is dissolved.
2. Put the indigo into a dye saucepan with a little water and stir to a paste.
3. Add 5oz of the soda and water mixture to the indigo paste and stir well. (Surplus soda mixture can be used as a 'booster' after the first dip).
4. Shake in 2oz of sodium hydrosulphite, add 2 pints of warm, soft water and heat to 125°F, stirring gently with a rod.
5. Stand in a warm place for thirty minutes, after which the liquid should be clear yellow if manufactured indigo is being used or greenish yellow if you are using natural polyganum indigo.
6. Shake 2oz of sodium hydrosulphite over the liquid; this completes the de-oxidisation.
7. Dip the clean wet wool into the liquid for five minutes. On lifting out this will emerge yellow and then turn green and finally blue in the air. Immerse and air repeatedly for equal lengths of time until the desired depth of colour is obtained.
8. Rinse in soft water containing 2 tablespoons of salt and 2 tablespoons of vinegar, which counteract a tendency to 'bleed'.
9. Wash and rinse again. Dry in the shade.

The Dye-Bearing Polygonums

Until very recently the use of *Polygonum tinctorium*, *Polygonum chinense* and *Polygonum aviculare* (dyer's knotweed) as a source of indigo was confined to the Far East, mainly to Japan and the coasts of China. The great revival of interest in natural dyeing over the last decade has led to the re-examination of this most useful group of plants and they are now cultivated by a number of dyers in the British Isles and the USA. Weight for weight, *Polygonum tinctorium* yields far more colour than woad, but being a tropical plant it requires heat, probably not much below 60°F, for survival; in this country therefore, the seeds must be sown in March or April and the plants kept indoors until all danger of frost is past. In the northern hemisphere the plants may be brought to flowering point in the garden during a hot dry summer, but I have never succeeded in persuading them to seed out of doors. If seed is required, the plants must be potted and brought into the house. The seeds, which form from November to March, should be removed individually from the flower heads, as they open, with a pair of tweezers. Not all the seeds mature at once, and it is a weekly job to collect them during the flowering period. The seeds are very similar to those of our common and pale persicarias, as are the plants themselves.

Plants sown in April and transplanted out of doors in mid-June will be ready for cutting for use in dyeing in late August or early September. Apart from the section grown for seed, all the tops of the plants are picked or cut; sometimes if they are cut early they will sprout again, so it is advisable never to pull up the whole plant until the first frosts have turned the remaining leaves blue and dry, for these too may be used for dyeing. The leaves may be used three ways: fresh from the plant, frozen in plastic bags in the freezer or dried like herbs and stored in paper bags. It is also possible to treat fresh indigo leaves like woad by making an alkaline solution from them before storing, with a teaspoonful of sodium metabisulphite as a preservative, in large air-tight containers. The solution will keep for at least two years without deterioration and may be used at any time. It is a particularly useful method of storing indigo for teaching and demonstrations when large quantities of dye liquid may be needed. Plastic gallon vinegar containers (well washed) serve excellently for this purpose. The container should be filled so that it almost overflows.

In Japan, until very recently, polygonum leaves were cut before the plants flowered and spread out in the sun to dry. They were then laid on the floor of a special room and watered, in much the same way as woad balls were crushed and watered on woad farms in the Fens. Fermentation set in after watering and *Bacillus indigogenous* converted the dry leaves into a dark blue mass which was made into balls after being well pounded and mixed together. For dyeing these balls were dissolved in alkaline water in pots containing lime, soda ash, bran and wood ash and stirred occasionally until a froth with blue tints began to form. More lime and bran were added and the whole dyebath was left to ferment for two weeks. Yarn or cloth was dipped in the clear yellow solution and then aired. The longer the dipping and airing, the darker the colour became.

The reader will note the similarity of method between dyeing with fresh indigofera or polygonum leaves and fresh woad leaves with the following difference. Indigofera and polygonum leaves contain an enzyme, liberated at a temperature of 122°F, which removes a glucose which is combined with the indoxyl. Fresh indigo and polygonum leaves are therefore always put into *cold* soft water and heated slowly to 120°F with a lid on the saucepan, whereas woad leaves are *scalded* with nearly boiling water and cooled to 120°F before use. In both cases the leaves are strained and discarded from the solution, which is then used for direct dyeing with whichever reduction agent and solvent the dyer may prefer.

Nerium tinctorium

The oleander or rosebay (*Nerium tinctorium* or *Nerium oleander*) grows in a wide belt stretching from the Mediterranean across the Near and Middle East to India, China and Japan, where it has been cultivated for centuries. Common in the wadis of the Holy Land as a wild shrub, its leaves have been likened to olive: hence its name. Cultivated in Western Europe for at least three hundred years, oleanders are popular house plants with pink or occasionally white flowers. Travellers in the eighteenth century reported that near inhabited places *Nerium tinctorium* was often cut for firewood, but that when it was allowed to grow to its full height it reached from 11 to 15ft.

For dyeing the shrub was cut low like the silkworm mulberry to encourage a prolific growth of leaves which were picked towards the end of April when at their best, though they could be gathered throughout the summer until the end of August. The method of extracting the indigo from the leaves was to scald them for about three hours and then to agitate the liquid to promote oxidation. About 1lb of indigo could be extracted from 200 to 300lb of nerium leaves, so that it compared favourably as a dye source with the indigoferas and polygonums and was much higher-yielding than woad.

All parts of *Nerium tinctorium* contain a poisonous white milk or latex and should be handled with care. The latex is used in medicine for its glucosides.

Marsdenia

Mr Marsden, in his history of Sumatra, records an indigo-bearing plant which appears to be peculiar to that island. The natives call it tarroom akkar, but to us it is known as marsdenia after its discoverer. Marsdenia is a vine-like creeping plant with dark green laurel-shaped leaves from 4 to 5 ins. long.

The native method of extracting the dye from this plant was to soak and macerate the stalks and branches for some days in water, which was then boiled and mixed with quicklime. A species of fern was employed for fixing the colour. After this the liquid was used for direct dyeing, dipping and airing until the desired depth of blue was reached. The Sumatran method of obtaining and using indigo direct from the plant without a concentration process is a recognizable link with the remote past when all other indigo-bearing species were treated in a similar manner.

Lonchocarpus

In western Nigeria an indigo-producing shrub known as *Lonchocarpus cyanescens* is used for dyeing blue on cotton. In the north of the country the dyeing is done by men, but in the west it is always carried out by women, many of whom begin learning at the age of ten or thereabouts. Dyeing is quite laborious as the whole process is carried out in sequence, the woman preparing her own ash from the local weeds and picking and pounding the Lonchocarpus leaves before making them into large balls. The wood ash is also made into balls by mixing with water, and after drying they are stored, like the dye balls, until they are needed. Dyeing is always carried out in the shade and the vats are sunk in the ground. The dyers sit on low walls as they work.

To prepare the dye vat, the lonchocarpus leaf balls are broken up and dropped in and then

Extracting indigo from lonchocarpus near Kano. (Jill Goodwin.)

covered with ash water. The vat is covered closely for up to three days and left unstirred. When the indigo begins to ferment small dark greenish blue bubbles rise to the surface. The yarn or cloth is completely immersed and left to absorb the indigo. Dipping and airing goes on until the dyer obtains the shade of blue she requires. So strong is the concentration of colour that the cloth is never squeezed or rinsed; it is folded and beaten with a wooden mallet until it is pressed smooth. The dye pours out of the cloth when it is first washed but this appears to be of no consequence to the dyers who assert that it will take years of exposure to sunlight to reduce it to a pale colour.

Woad

In temperate climates the first and foremost of the indigo-bearing dye plants is woad (*Isatis tinctoria*; *Isatis indigotina*), and it is the most neglected. Nearly every dye book which has been published since commercial woad production ceased in the British Isles in 1932 dismisses it as a dye plant of the past and of little except historic interest to modern dyers. Nothing could be further from the truth. Today we need dye plants which are not only hardy and suitable for our climate but which are also cheaply and easily grown and which will provide good, strong, fast colours. Woad fulfils all these conditions perfectly and on these grounds alone it is due for a permanent revival.

Indigenous to Assyria, western Asia and the countries surrounding the Mediterranean Sea, woad spread by the movements and migrations of mankind until by historic times it was to be found in every European country and in Scandinavia as far north as the point at which the winters become severe. In Great Britain the last large stand of fully naturalized woad is to be found on a cliff called the Mythe, on the banks of the River Severn just outside Tewkesbury. Occasionally the traveller who has his eyes on the verges instead of the road may see woad growing in small clumps in the fenland areas of East Anglia. Apart from where it is cultivated by dyers it is rarely grown in any quantity, but gardeners and flower arrangers like it for its abundant yellow blooms in the spring, its pale green seed cases in June and its purple pendulous fruits in late summer, which may also be dried for winter arrangements.

The last transplanting of woad to another country took place when the Pilgrim Fathers fled to North America. Along with seeds and food plants, well-known dye plants were shipped with the emigrants. Even in the severe winters of Maine and Boston the plants survived and rapidly spread as the country was developed by the settlers. Until the southern stands of indigo in Florida and Carolina were discovered, woad was the only dye plant which gave fast blues on wool and cotton.

Early dyers have left us fewer written records about the way in which they used woad than about many other plants. It is difficult to tell at what point in history dyers abandoned the use of a solution of freshly picked woad leaves and progressed to picking and crushing the leaves before compressing them into large balls for drying and storage. The change of method would have evolved with the need for handling large quantities of plant leaf and of preserving them in a form in which they could be stored. Admittedly the yield of indigo from woad leaves is low compared with the same weight of material from the indigoferas or the polyganums: at least four times the weight of woad leaves is required to produce the same depth of colour.

The bulky nature of the plant influenced the woad growers of the Middle Ages. It was a labour-intensive crop and required much hand cultivation. At the time of peak production, just before the first indigo was imported into Great Britain in the sixteenth century, woad was grown in Somerset, Lincolnshire and East Anglia and in several other counties with deep rich soil. As in the

Fenland 'waddies' balling crushed woad. (Wisbech and Fenland Museum.)

fermentation of indigo, the woad vats were pungent and evil-smelling. Queen Elizabeth I objected so strongly to this that she issued a decree which forbade the processing of woad within five miles of the royal estates; nor would she travel anywhere near towns or other centres where woad was being prepared for dyeing. Had she lived for another century she would have witnessed the decline of the once-great woad industry, for indigo was soon introduced into Europe by the Dutch East India company and after much resistance and legislation the 'king of dyestuffs' supplanted and finally displaced woad. Dyers soon discovered that indigo was cheaper, less bulky to handle and gave brighter and clearer blues but that its colour was not as fast, and on this count woad was retained and used in conjunction with indigo in the dye vats to provide both good colour and durability.

Thus it was that, by the end of the nineteenth century, when natural indigo was itself challenged by the newly discovered synthetic indigo, woad had declined to the point where only three or four farms were still growing it in the Fens of East Anglia. From this last remaining stronghold the leaves were picked and then crushed by huge stone rollers pulled by heavy horses. The pulpy, mustard-smelling mass was balled by men known as 'waddies' and dried on racks open at the sides to currents of air. Later the balls were again crushed, this time to a powder under the same rollers, and fermented in a heap on the floor of the 'couching house' until they had become a clay-like powder, similar in appearance to the indigo noted by Marco Polo in Coulan. The blue powder was packed into barrels and sent off to Yorkshire for use in the dye houses attached to the woollen mills, there to be used as a fermenting agent in the indigo vats. Until 1932 woad was included in the vats used for dyeing the uniforms of the British police force. A typical recipe of this period is as follows:

15kg indigo
300kg woad
10kg bran
2.15kg madder
12kg slaked lime (very freshly made)

During the entire nineteenth and early twentieth centuries woad exercised a curious fascination over men of science as well as over practical dyers. Francis Darwin visited the Parsons Drove woad mill near Wisbech in 1896 and wrote an account of the harvesting and drying procedures for the magazine *Nature*. He considered that breaking down the woad balls and fermenting them with water resulted 'in a zymolitic decomposition of glucosides'.

Professor M. W. Beyerinck held the view that all the indigo-bearing plants could be divided into two groups, one consisting of the indigoferas and the polygonums which contained indican, and the other consisting of woad which contained indoxyl. Later he came to the conclusion that a loose compound which he called isatan was present in woad. This was broken down into indoxyl by an enzyme known as isatase.

The last surviving relics of the woad industry are to be found today as place names for roads, schools and fields in Cambridgeshire and Lincolnshire. A few woad plants still flourish at the sides of fields and ditches in these areas and they also can be seen in collections in botanic gardens and agricultural colleges. However, over the last decade a revival of interest in woad has taken place and there is now a demand for seeds and plants from the few people who grow it on a larger scale.

Dyers who enthusiastically grow and use woad for the first time without knowing anything about the plant are dismayed when they obtain pinks, buffs, browns and dirty greens from the leaves, instead of the beautiful blues which they confidently expect. My post bag is full of laments from these poor souls but I hope that after reading this chapter they will take heart and proceed happily ever after to produce the colour they so much desire.

One of the first facts of English history which children learn at school is that the ancient Britons dyed themselves blue with a plant called woad. Caesar in his *De Bello Gallico* (Book 5, Chapter 14) clearly states that they did. Pliny records a plantain-like plant called *glastum* with which the wives and daughters of the Britons smeared themselves, 'being the colour of Ethiopeans'. Ovid speaks of our ancestors as *virides Britannos*. These three commentators differ, giving blue, black and green as the dye from woad. They were all correct, for each of these colours can be made from the leaves and many more besides.

The term woad is a derivative of the Anglo-Saxon *wad* or *waad*, from which the waddies of the Fens also gained their name. As recently as 1970 the few remaining survivors of this ancient breed were recorded on tape by Norman Wills of Long Sutton, and their reminiscences have been enshrined in his interesting book *Woad in the Fens*.

Woad was the great universal dye plant of the Middle Ages and was used for 'top' and 'bottom' dyeing a great many other colours. 'Bottom' dyeing is the first of two processes in which one colour is modified by the use of a second ('top' dyeing). Saxon green, with weld as the source of yellow dye, was produced in this way, as were Lincoln and Kendal greens, using either weld or broom leaves (*Genista tinctoria*). As the Roman writers quoted above bear witness, there are other colours in woad besides blue. If alum is added to woad-leaf solution after the blue dye has been extracted from it, wool can be dyed a pleasing soft pink which is complementary to the blue and mixes well with it.

I have used woad as a dye plant for nearly twenty years and have never failed to obtain blue from the first-year leaves between mid-June and early November. The weather will determine whether it can be picked and used in May or December. I have made hundreds of tests during the spring and summer months with not only the maincrop first-year leaves which contain the bulk of the dye, but also with the yellow flowers and purple fruits of the second-year growth, and with the second-year leaves before the plants run to seed, when the soft lavenders and violet greys disappear. One is left with the conclusion that woad is an extremely useful and versatile plant, indispensable to the new generation of dyers with gardens, for with weld and madder growing alongside one has the three primary colours from which an infinite number of colour mixtures can be made. Thomas Fuller, writing in the seventeenth century, described woad as 'color and colorem, the stock whereon other colours are grafted. Yes, it giveth them truth and fruitfulness who without it prove failing and hypocritical.'

'THE GREAT WOAD HUNT'

The reader may be entertained by an account of learning to use woad the hard way, which became known in the author's family as 'The Great Woad Hunt'. Apart from the knowledge that woad was an extremely valuable dye plant much used by the Britons, I knew nothing of it until, in 1962, a friend sent me some seeds from a garden in Hertfordshire. Sown in August, the seeds grew into large plants which were ready for use the following July. I picked half the leaves and simmered them for an hour before straining them and using the liquid with a range of mordants as one would with any unknown dye plant. There was no sign of blue, but I got a curious collection of pinks, auburns, fawns and olive greens. Using all the remaining leaves, I combined some of the mordants, still with the same results, and was obliged to admit defeat. The most sensible thing seemed to be to apply to the fountain head for enlightenment and a letter to the British Museum Science Laboratory brought forth rich fruit in a recommendation to read Dr J. B. Hurry's book *The Woad Plant and its Dye*. Though this classic work was out of print for many years it is now available again (see Bibliography) and I strongly recommend it to all serious students of woad dyeing. It told me practically everything I wished to know about the plant and the industry which grew up round it except for a simple method of extracting the blue dye from the leaves, but there were two vital paragraphs. The first stated: 'In Medieval times a solution of woad, with alum or potash as a mordant, was put in a container and heated to a high temperature for three hours. The material was then immersed and dyed. The longer it was left in the dyebath the deeper the colour would be. The scum at the top of the bath was used to colour paint by artists.' This bald statement unfortunately did not have the qualification it badly needed. There was no mention of the quantity of mordant, or the stage at which it was added, or the manner in which it was used.

The second and more valuable pointer was a reference to an article by Dr Plowright, written for the journal of the Royal Horticultural Society in 1901. This outlined a simple method of extracting the indican by infusing fresh woad leaves in almost-boiling water, the lid being kept tightly on the vessel for at least thirty minutes to exclude air and prevent oxidation. At the end of this time the leaves were strained off and the sherry-coloured fluid divided into several jars, each one containing a different alkali. Lime water, washing soda, ammonia and caustic potash were used, though baking soda, very dilute caustic soda (though bad for wool) or stale (two-week-old) urine would all have been effective. The sherry-coloured woad juice turned dark green inside each jar after stirring, and this was used for dyeing wool directly, by dipping and airing over an extended period.

I felt so inspired by this article that I doubled the area of the woad in my garden and in due course when the leaves were ready I began dyeing operations on an ambitious scale, only to find to my intense disappointment that the wool dyed by Dr Plowright's simple method, though a beautiful blue, was not fast to soap when it was washed, the first necessity for any dye. I pondered for weeks and at last wondered if, having leached out the dye material from the leaves, it might be treated in a similar manner to indigo. After much trial and error this line of thought finally proved successful. I knew that the Scottish Highlanders used lumps of indigo brought back from the Far East by their sailors and that they obtained fast blue dyes by putting the indigo into a vessel containing stale urine and heating the dyebath by dropping a stone hot from the fire into the brew. When the solution became cool they would add another hot stone, continuing over a period of several days. The heat induced fermentation of the indigo and urine and the insoluble indoxyl was converted to indigo white. A practical test with this method showed that the scalding stone raised the temperature of the dyebath to 120°F, the optimum for fermentation. Wool or yarn was simply dipped and aired until the colour was as dark as was required. Sorrel roots were used in solution to fix the dye and prevent 'bleeding' of the indigo.

The answer to my woad problem seemed to lie in making a solution of fresh leaves, adding an alkali — wood ash, soda or ammonia (all cheap) — beating the green liquid well to obtain the maximum blue dye by oxidation, dipping and airing the wool to dye it and then, once it was dyed, fixing the colour permanently by soaking the wool in stale urine for up to two weeks at a warm temperature. This procedure was so successful and so simple that I was able to recommend it to some research workers who were interested in dyeing with woad by a method likely to have been used in the Iron Age. Later still I discovered that once the woad juice and alkali had been well whisked together it was possible to obtain splendid blues in three days simply by adding a handful of bran to the bath and fermenting it in a warm place.

From knowing nothing about woad initially I began to collect a great deal of practical information from others who were interested in its potential as a blue dye. A scientist in Cambridge carefully explained to me the chemical changes which take place during the infusion and dyeing process, and he also told me of other ways of treating home-grown woad and indigo, all of which proved successful. This advice came when it was most needed and I might have given up in frustration but for his help and encouragement. He too had reached the conclusion that knowledge should be shared, and his example has prompted me to write this book.

The Great Woad Hunt ended when I had evolved half a dozen different ways of using the leaves and getting good blues from all of them. By that time I was amazed that so little was known or had been recorded about all the ferments and fixing agents that I had been forced to re-discover for myself.

CULTIVATION

Woad is a cruciferous biennial which grows up to 5ft high in rich soil. In its first year of growth the leaves form a rosette of blue-green leaves which are similar in appearance to spinach. These are the leaves which are used for dyeing, although some colour is still present when the plant shoots into a flowering stem in April. The flower stem is stout and branching with clusters of bright mustard-yellow flowers which eventually turn into blue-black fruits.

Woad seed may be sown at any time of the year

Woad seeds strung up to dry. (Enid Tivey.)

Woad in flower. (Ray Harwood.)

First-year woad leaves. (Ray Harwood.)

when the soil is warm, which usually means from March to late October or early November. Germination is rapid and the plants may be sown in rows like cabbages and pricked out and transplanted when 2–4 ins. in height, or sown *in situ* at a thinner rate. Allow one plant for 9 sq.ins. of ground. Woad springs from a strong tap root so the sooner it is transplanted after the four-leaf stage the better it will grow without a check. October-sown seed will produce leaves fit for dye-

Harvesting woad seeds. (Ray Harwood.)

81

ing from the following June onwards, while seed sown in March will mature in late summer and be fit for picking before the first sharp frosts. If you have a large enough garden, it is useful to make two different sowings so that there is always a supply of fresh leaves in prime condition.

As a crop wood can be picked four or five times during the summer and autumn and a good strong soil will yield up to a ton of fresh leaves per acre. The plants must be kept well hoed and allowed plenty of room for development and a number of plants may be saved for seed each year. Mark the biggest and strongest plants bearing the most seed (the two go together) for this purpose so that the selection of high-yielding strains is continuous.

The greatest amount of colour is present in woad leaves in midsummer, from late July to early September. At this time of the year it is possible to ferment the leaves out of doors in the sunshine. This would have been the season when the plants were used in prehistoric times, though I have extracted good blues from woad leaves as late as mid-December if the autumn has been mild, by fermenting them in cartons on the side of my Aga cooker.

As woad flowers in April and early May, the fruits are sufficiently ripe for harvesting in July and August, when they are cut with bean hooks and stacked in upright bunches to dry off and mature. The seeds are rubbed off the stalks by hand, for which a pair of stout gardening gloves should be worn, over a seed sieve of the correct dimensions.

The seed of woad will germinate for up to five years after harvesting provided that it is left in the outer black casing. The crop should be stored in strong paper or linen sacks, never in plastic. For successful storage the fruits should be bone dry before bagging.

THE CHEMISTRY OF WOAD

Woad leaves contain indican in the form of an ester of indoxyl. By means of an enzyme in the leaves, or with alkalis, this can be broken down to give indigo white, which may then be treated by the hydrosulphite vat or by fermentation. The three vital points to remember when using woad are:

1. Use only *soft* water. No blues may be obtained with hard water, only pinks.
2. Never allow the fermentation temperature to exceed 125°F or much of the blue will be lost.
3. Discard the woad leaves after squeezing them well following half an hour's infusion. By then the indoxyl will all be in the infused liquid.

PRESERVATION AND STORAGE

Experiments with woad leaves at every stage of their growth show that practically all the colour is lost if the leaves are dried like herbs, and that frozen leaves are little better. Three other methods of storing woad for winter use therefore remain:

1. Store as large balls of minced, compressed leaf – the method used on the woad farms. I personally never use this method as it is too wasteful of the blue dye, but it is convenient when really large quantities of leaf must be stored, and the balls can be augmented with some polyganum or indigofera leaves, also balled and dried, to achieve a good colour.
2. Store as a liquid. Woad indigo may be stored successfully for several years in this form if prepared according to the instructions which follow.
3. Store as a powder. Make a solution, beat the sherry-coloured juice with an alkali, filter the sediment and dry it as blue indigo powder. This is a very fiddly process and nothing like as convenient as method 2 which requires only a reducing agent to produce a dyebath in half an hour. The only advantage of method 3 is that it takes up much less storage space.

To Make Woad Solution for Storage
1. Make an infusion of fresh woad leaves with nearly boiling soft water in a container with a tightly fitting lid. Add the water so that a little overflows to exclude all the air.
2. After thirty to forty minutes, strain off the sherry-coloured fluid.
3. Add an alkali – wood-ash liquid (see below for instructions for making this), washing soda, ammonia or caustic potash. Beat the mixture very thoroughly until the peacock blue froth on the surface turns dark green – this should take about five minutes.
5. Pour the liquid into an airtight container, filling it completely.
6. Add 1 teaspoonful of sodium metabisulphite (as a preservative) to the container and screw the lid down.

To Prepare Wood-ash Liquid
Wood ash is prepared for use as a mordant by placing it in a container of soft water, stirring it well with a clean stick and leaving it to settle for several days. The clear liquid, strongly alkaline, is removed from above the ash without disturbing it.

TO DYE WITH FRESH WOAD LEAVES

Three methods of dyeing with fresh woad leaves are given in this section, though there are others. The first two will appeal to those people who have a taste for simple low-cost techniques and who are averse to spending money on chemicals when natural alternatives are available. As regards quantities, remember that 1lb of woad leaves will dye 2oz of wool. The methods are:

1. The ancient method.
2. The soda fermentation vat. This gives bright clear colours.
3. The hydrosulphite vat. This is expensive compared with methods 1 and 2.

1. *The Ancient Method*
In July or August pick a saucepanful of woad leaves and tear them into small pieces. Scald them with nearly boiling soft water. Place a close-fitting lid on the saucepan after you have filled it to overflowing. Leave for thirty to forty minutes, then strain off the sherry-coloured fluid for the dyebath and squeeze the leaves dry before discarding them. (Alternatively you can simmer the used leaves with alum to obtain a pink dye.) Pour the dye liquid into a bowl and add enough wood-ash liquor to turn the solution dark green. If you have no wood ash, use washing soda or ammonia. Whisk the mixture for at least five minutes to aerate it well. Have ready a plastic 1gal container half-filled with stale urine to which 1 cupful of bran has been

Preparing woad solution for storage. (Ray Harwood.)

added. Add the woad solution and clean wet wool and screw the lid on. Set the carton in full sunshine for at least two weeks, or if the weather is cool put it in a haybox or warm place so that it is kept at nearly 125°F for several days. After fermenting, air the wool twice daily until it is as dark as required. Rinse in salt soft water. Wash and rinse at least twice. Dry in the open air out of direct sunlight. This old method of dyeing with woad is very cheap, easy and foolproof and leaves the wool in a very good condition.

A

2. *The Soda Fermentation Vat*
This method is suitable for owners of solid-fuel cookers or a really warm airing cupboard; it is cheap and gives very good peacock blue colours. The smell is strong, and airing and uncovering the wool is therefore best done out of doors. Pick and tear up enough fresh woad leaves to fill a large plastic carton. Cover with warm soft water in which 2 tablespoonfuls of soda have been dissolved. Cover the container very tightly and leave in a warm place for twenty-four hours at a temperature of 95–110°F. The following day remove and squeeze the woad leaves and add 2 cupfuls of bran to the dyebath. Add the clean wet wool or yarn and return to the warmth to ferment. Twenty-four hours later remove and air the wool for ten minutes; it should now be a beautiful *eau de nil* green. Replace the wool and keep in the warm. Air out of doors on the following day as the mixture will begin to smell strong. Very little colour will be taken up by the wool after the fifth or sixth day. Remove and rinse in soft water. Wash and rinse twice, changing the water for the second washing.

B

3. *The Hydrosulphite Vat*
Pick 1½lb of fresh woad leaves and tear them into small pieces. Scald the leaves with 2½ gals of nearly boiling soft water. Allow the leaves to infuse for thirty minutes. Strain off the liquid and squeeze all the juice from the leaves. Add enough

C

84

Opposite and above: Dyeing with woad using the hydrosulphite vat. (Ray Harwood.)

A Preparing to strain off the sherry-coloured liquid after infusing the woad leaves.
B Adding the washing soda.
C Whisking.
D Adding the sodium hydrosulphite.
E Adding the clean, wet wool to the now yellow-green liquid.
F Airing the wool. The colour change from yellow to green is clearly visible, with blue developing at the top of the skein.
G The dyeing is complete: the skein is a fully developed blue.

in our household we have two favourite lichen-dyed Harris tweed coats which have survived in hard wear for over half a century and which still emit their pungent aroma of Crottle or Scrottytie, as the lichen is known locally, particularly when they are damp.

I once spent a fruitful afternoon scraping and bagging a large sackful of the orange lichen *Xanthoria parietina* off the roof of the barn of a farming friend. The barn had collapsed in a gale and was going to be pulled down so that the lichen would have been destroyed in any case; this rich harvest lasted for many months and dyed several pounds of wool pink and red after the lichen had been soaked in washing soda and ammonia for a week or two and fermented in cartons on the side of my Aga cooker. When using this recipe you will note that after the soda and ammonia have been soaking for two days the colour begins to run like blackberry juice; if, however, a little distilled vinegar or acetic acid is added on the fourth day the colour seems to brighten.

The lichens which produce reds and pinks and purples on fermentation are very economical in use and as the result of many practical experiments I would strongly query the often-quoted allowance of equal weights of dyestuff and fibre, though this *is* the right amount for brown and yellow lichens. Good strong colours depend as much or more on the quality of the water used in dyeing and whether chalk is present in it. Half the weight of red-producing lichen to wool will give excellent results. Red-producing lichens can of course also be boiled, but only browns are obtained by this method which seems therefore rather wasteful.

The Scottish Highlanders traditionally made a 'contact' dye by packing their pots with a layer of wool and a layer of lichen before simmering with soft water, to produce brown, yellow and orange shades. With the red-producing lichens they packed the dyebath with clean wet wool, lichen and stale urine and fermented the batch with heat for upwards of a month or even longer for dark

Wonderfully brilliant pinks can be obtained from this insignificant-looking lichen, Ochrolechia tartarea. *In the background is a crocheted jerkin of wool dyed with different dippings of this lichen and woad. (Ray Harwood.)*

A fine example of the lichen Xanthoria parietina *growing on a wall. (Enid Tivey.)*

colours. The wool was aired twice daily for about half an hour to allow the colour to develop.

The main forms of lichen growth are:

1. Crustose: those which form a crust on the surface to which they are attached – trees, rocks and other fairly hard surfaces.
2. Fruticose: those which resemble a small hair-like shrub (erect or pendulous) and which grow on wood, bog plants or rock.
3. Foliose: those which are leafy and flat, which are usually attached to their growing place by a number of points or at a single central point. They are found on trees, fences, rocks and mosses and are luxuriant in growth at lower altitudes.

For dyeing, lichens fall into four categories:

1. Those that yield no dye by any method.
2. Those that yield colour by boiling only – usually yellows, browns and oranges.
3. Those that will ferment with washing soda and ammonia (or stale urine) to give reds, blues and purples.
4. Those that will yield different colours with boiling and fermentation.

Lichen dyes are substantive (needing no mordant) and they are extremely fast to light, washing and salt water. Only a few hours of simmering are necessary to extract and attach the colours. With lichens which give colour on boiling only the general rule is to allow equal weights of wool and dyestuff and to submerge both in sufficient water to cover completely before simmering gently for one to three hours.

SOME LICHENS WHICH YIELD RED, BLUE OR PURPLE

Evernia prunastri

This, the ragged hoary or stag's horn lichen, is found on trees in old orchards. Its smell is very strong, like chloride of lime, which is a help in identification. Fermented with ammonia, it gives a rich plum colour; with boiling, a deep brown.

Ochrolechia tartarea

Formerly known as *Leconora tartarea*, this lichen is usually found on rocks in upland areas and sometimes on trees, and resembles a tiny cauliflower in form. It is much used in Wales, the Orkney and Shetland Islands and in Scotland. A preparation of *Ochrolechia tartarea* is known as archil in England, litmus in Holland, and in Scotland cudbear after Dr Cuthbert Gordon who evolved the method of preparation. Scottish crofters prepare a dye by first drying and crushing the lichen to a fine powder and soaking it in stale urine for several weeks before mixing it with chalk or powdered shells and forming it into balls for storage. These are boiled with alum to give dark red colours. The colour from *Ochrolechia tartarea* is so bright that a local bishop who was opening an Essex school quite recently and who inspected a display of spinning and dyeing which the children had mounted, commented on the purple colour of some wool dyed with it and held it up to compare it with his silk vestment. The two colours were identical and matched as exactly as if they had been dyed in the same dyebath.

Xanthoria parietina

This is the common yellow wall lichen often found on walls and fences and also on trees. It was formerly called *Parmelia parietina*. With wool which has first been mordanted with bichromate of potash, *Xanthoria parietina* will yield pinks with long simmering. At some seasons of the year, when there is bright sunlight, the pinks will turn blue on exposure to the midday sun. This lichen thrives on barn roofs near stockyards where there is ammonia in the atmosphere, and it is best gathered from the south side of buildings which have been exposed to sunlight. *Xanthoria parietina* also gives good gold and brown colours on simmering in soft water.

Parmelia saxatilis

This is the lichen, known locally as Crottle or Scrottytie, which imparts the characteristic aroma to Harris tweed. Cloth dyed with it will retain the smell indefinitely. Found growing on rocks, trees and walls in grey rosettes, it is best gathered in August after a wet period. *Parmelia saxatilis* will give fine reds or purples after fermentation with stale urine or with soda and ammonia, and browns on simmering in soft water (see page 91).

Umbilicaria pustulata

When wet this lichen is bright olive green in appearance, and it feels like jelly, but on drying it turns to grey or brown, with 'blisters' (hence its name). *Umbilicaria pustulata* is found on rocks at high altitudes in mountainous areas; it is known to Arctic explorers as 'rock tripe' and may be used as a food in emergency situations. Not much of this lichen should be gathered at a time, and it should not be gathered when it is immature, for it spreads slowly and is not plentiful. It is economical in use and will produce good dark reds with ammonia. *Umbilicaria pustulata* should be very carefully dried before storage as it behaves like seaweed and attracts moisture.

Ochrolechia parella
This is known as crawfish or crab's eye lichen because of its protruding fruits. The grey variety seems to give more colour than the white. *Ochrolechia parella* was much used by the Scottish Highlanders to produce the oranges and reds for certain tartans. A dye was made from it in France which was known as *orseille d'Auvergne*. On long maceration with ammonia or stale urine, *Ochrolechia parella* yields wine red.

Rocella tinctoria
Found on the shores of the Mediterranean Sea and the Canary Islands, this lichen is interesting historically as it was used to produce the nearest equivalent to royal purple after the collapse of the Phoenician dye ports of Tyre and Sidon.

Cladonia impexa
This lichen contains usnic acid and is tinged yellow. The general appearance is grey and hair-like. It grows in dense cushions in heather and among moss on moors, particularly in Devon and Cornwall. On maceration with ammonia, *Cladonia impexa* will give shades of pink and red.

SOME LICHENS WHICH YIELD YELLOW, ORANGE AND BROWN ON LONG SIMMERING WITH SOFT WATER

Hypogymnia physodes
Formerly known as *Parmelia physodes*, and commonly called dark crottle, this lichen which thrives in damp conditions is found on rocks and in woods where it may be seen hanging on trees. It yields fine golden browns on simmering with soft water.

Parmelia omphalodes
This lichen, black crottle, is found in Wales, Scotland, Scandinavia and in parts of the USA on rocks at high altitudes. It is cushion-like and wide-spreading, with dark brown and purple lobes. With boiling water it will give purples which are faster than those obtained from *Ochrolechia tartarea*.

Lobaria pulmonaria
This lichen is olive green and flaccid when wet, and yellow, brown and stiff when dry. It appears rag-like and dark green to black when it is old. Common to Great Britain, Scandinavia and the Great Lakes area of America, it is found on old trees, particularly the oak, and on rocks. The Hereford stocking makers used *Lobaria pulmonaria* to make a strong brown dye for their hose. As it is very slow-growing it should be harvested only in small quantities. A century ago it was used for making into a jelly for invalids suffering from lung infections for which it was supposed to be a remedy.

Parmelia saxatilis
This lichen, described on page 90, will give very rich red browns by simmering in soft water. (On fermentation with ammonia it yields bright reds.)

It appears to me as a practical dyer that we must discover or re-discover many fresh dye plants for ourselves. The lichens are a vast source of dye material which has only ever been partially tapped. As so many lichens look alike to the layman it is as well to have one's collection identified by an expert before beginning operations, and the plants can then be very carefully labelled for future reference.

Dyeing in Schools 11

Dyeing is one of the processes of textile production and in some schools, both primary and secondary, it is taught as part of the history or art curriculum. Unfortunately, in many schools dyeing is not taught at all, although it is as primary a process as pottery, painting or basketry. I look forward to the day when every school will have the means of teaching all the skills which man has developed from earliest times, so that children may see themselves as part of a continuously evolving process and grow up learning to use their hands as well as their brains.

I have taught spinning and dyeing in all kinds of schools, going as a catalyst for a day or two wherever there has been a need for specialized instruction. On each occasion I was asked to the school because either a member of the staff or a group of children wished it. Sometimes the visit

The author instructing a class. (Monega Art Centre.)

Opposite: Unspun wool dyed many different shades with woad. Note the enormous colour variation from pale blue to almost navy. (Ray Harwood.)

Gathering sorrel. (Monega Art Centre.)

was the culmination and crystallization of months of work in the school; at other times it was the beginning of a year of school work on spinning, dyeing or weaving.

I have found that the facilities of a school have little to do with the success of such a visit: the vital ingredient has always been the keenness and enthusiasm of the teacher and the children.

The chief difficulty which besets the teaching of any kind of handicraft in schools today is the lack of time and money. But these are problems which may be overcome with care and thought. It is now considered desirable that school buildings should be used for as many hours a day as possible, and when the school day is over they are usually available for evening classes run by local authorities. There is also a period in the dinner hour and another following afternoon school when it is possible to organize groups of children for activities within the school buildings. Even thirty minutes to an hour once or twice a week will result in a lot of work over a school term or year. In one school where I taught once a week for eight months, the group of children explored a wide selection of local plants, growing some in the school garden and collecting others from their own gardens and the surrounding fields. Having dyed the yarns which they had spun on hand spindles that they had made themselves, they mounted an exhibition at the end of the year and spent an

The class washing hanks of wool which they have spun themselves. (Monega Art Centre.)

afternoon demonstrating their skills as illustration to a talk I was giving to a science society whose members came from every part of the country.

As for funds, the aim of all handicraft teachers should be to 'live off the land' as much as possible. This means enlisting parental help and support. The modern trend is to involve parents fully in the life of the school where their children are pupils, so that a pool of skills and resources is available, varying greatly in different areas but, like the water table, always there as an 'underground' source of nourishment. Parents are now well aware that such common necessities as textbooks and writing paper are increasingly expensive and that materials for arts and crafts are regarded as luxuries and tend to be squeezed out of the school budget. This is where parental help becomes invaluable. In one school a plea for dye materials brought forth such a response that it took the children six months to use the wealth of offerings from their homes. In the bags and baskets which arrived were flower heads of all kinds, twigs and shrub prunings; soot from a kitchen chimney which dyed wool orange and not black as the child expected; cochineal, turmeric, mustard, tea and coffee from kitchen cupboards; and purple cabbages, berries, carrot tops and onion skins from gardens.

Without the opportunity to experiment which my brothers and I enjoyed as children this book would probably never have been written. Because

Gathering leaves from second-year flowering woad plants. (Monega Art Centre.)

we were encouraged to look closely at plants and animals very early in life we found learning to be a continuous process, one thing leading to another. Nobody suggested to us that we should dye our wool collection with windfall damsons, make sun-baked bricks in tobacco tins or construct rough baskets or clay pots. A very strong primitive instinct prompted us and when we followed it our days were long and happy. The joy which comes from making things for oneself is the right of every child and no school timetable is complete if practical subjects are sacrificed in favour of academic ones.

Dyeing in schools is an excellent way in which to introduce children to a multitude of other interests and it may be started at a very early age and continued to an advanced level in secondary schools and colleges. Many children who have started spinning and dyeing in their primary school have developed an interest in textiles which enriches their lives as well as assisting in their understanding of history and art. The amount of ground covered in the classroom will depend on the age of the children, the available time, and factors such as whether the school is situated in the country or in the town. An ambitious programme would include the following:

1. The study of natural fibres such as wool, silk, cotton, flax, nettles and mallow stems, and

the fur of cats, rabbits and dogs.

2. The different breeds of sheep found all over the world.

3. The work of the Rare Breeds Survival Trust. Visits to farm parks and zoos.

4. The life cycle of the silkworm and the treatment of the threads; the history of the silk trade and the silk routes through Asia.

5. The growth and treatment of cotton and flax historically and in modern times.

6. The methods and principles of spinning using spindles, the great wheel, flax wheels and home-made devices for spinning.

7. The clipping and grading of wool; shearing techniques.

8. Contrasted methods of preparing natural fibres for spinning and dyeing.

9. Dyeing fibres and spun yarn.

Taking the temperature of a dyebath to ensure that it does not exceed 120°F. (Monega Art Centre.)

The class proudly display items made from wool which they have dyed, spun and woven themselves – the result of six weeks' activity. (Monega Art Centre.)

10. The use of mordants; simple chemistry.
11. Using simple ferments for making vat dyes.
12. Constructing hand spindles and a simple great wheel.
13. Making backstrap looms, card looms and Inkle looms for braid weaving.
14. Rug making, including knotting and weaving techniques.
15. Botany; dye plants in use throughout the world.
16. Textile history; ancient methods of spinning and dyeing compared with those in use today.
17. Cultivating dye plants in the school garden.
18. Visits to local craft museums and botanic gardens.
19. Using a tape recorder to record dyeing experiments, and as a help in elocution and public speaking.
20. Mathematical calculations for threading looms.
21. How to use a flora, herbal and dictionary in tracking dye plants.
22. Painting plants used for dyeing.
23. Dissecting plants and studying their structure.
24. The history of clothes and garment design.
25. Making a video film of a set of dyeing experiments for the school resources bank.

In school groups of six children or more, each may work with a different mordant, so that if several plants are used as many as thirty different colour samples may be obtained in one lesson. Each group of children will have different potential and the skilled teacher is the one who senses quickly and draws the inherent talent from each child, making it feel that it has a unique contribution to make. Particular talents emerge as work progresses. I have known children who were fascinated by the mechanics of spinning and who decided to make a range of hand spindles from stone, clay, wood and plastic, calculating the weight and rate of spin of each substance. Others will whittle stirring rods for the dyepots or make backstrap looms from broom handles, using the school carpentry tools and work benches. Some children will enjoy sowing and growing dye plants in the school garden and one or two like gathering, drying and storing the harvest. I had one pupil who proved adept at mounting and displaying samples – she was a natural window dresser and mounted the greater part of a year's work with dyes in the school hall when it was officially opened by a local worthy. There are also a few exceptionally able and gifted children who will read every available textbook on dyeing and dismiss all the suggested dye sources, thinking of unlikely ones for themselves. They will adapt techniques and equipment to suit their needs, like the child I met who studied a home-made spinning wheel made from a bicycle wheel and promptly adapted the principle to a bobbin winder to make an excellent thread. These are children to watch and encourage particularly, for they are the innovators of tomorrow. How little we should advance if we lived without the freedom to experiment.

Children learn quickly that rubber gloves must be worn for the handling of mordants and that dyes must be used without splashing or spilling. If they are too young to use chemicals, the yarn must be premordanted by the teacher before the class begins. Children over nine are usually sensible enough to complete the dyeing process under close supervision.

I rarely take a school class in dyeing alone; it is usually part of a broader concept, embracing a study of fibres, yarns and plants, using the colours once they have been extracted and making small objects with the material each child achieves. The ways in which half a dozen different kinds of rug may be made will occupy one or two lessons, simple clothes construction another and wall hangings and tapestry weaving another.

Making felt from those parts of fleeces which are of the poorest quality never fails to fascinate children. Everyone enjoys taking a turn at pound-

The author shows the class how to make a simple spindle. (Monega Art Centre.)

ing the cotton-covered pad of layered wool in alternate boiling and cold water, with sprinkled soap flakes as the binding agent and a small mallet or potato masher as the tool. Shaping the felt into a hat on a pudding-basin mould using the steam from a boiling kettle is always fun. There will be a clamour to try on the result, and the promise of a clothes parade at the end of the school year inspires children to intense and continued effort.

Of course, access to a source of electricity and a sink with running water is greatly to be desired for ease of operating, but I have had to work in the most unlikely places at times and still produced lovely colours with the children, who regarded all the difficulties as a 'lark' and a challenge, never grumbling when there was no spare room and we had to work in the cloakrooms and passage or, in summer, in the school garden. In cases of extreme difficulty I have carted all but the kitchen sink in my car, including electric extension leads, portable two-burner electric rings and a large old-fashioned tin bath, as well as a range of saucepans for dyeing. Often in the summer it has been possible to make an outside fireplace from bricks and do all the dyeing out of doors – this is no bad thing when the brews are pungent, for powerful smells are taken in the stride of those who make them but they are not always appreciated by the rest of the school.

'As great oaks from tiny acorns grow,' one must always seize the opportunity to dye in schools. Often young adults who were formerly my pupils remind me of our long-forgotten experiments with dyes, particularly all the ones which went wrong! Obviously the appeal lies in the excitement of undertaking experiments for which the results are uncertain.

12 Using Dyed Fibres

The purpose of this chapter is not to make a detailed analysis of knitting and weaving techniques but rather to act as a pointer to the many ways in which home-spun hand-dyed fibres may be used – the ingenious readers will think of variations and adaptations for themselves. Many dyers know exactly what they wish to make with their yarns before they begin operations; others dye first and consider later, when they can see what quantity of each colour they have by them. Those who become enthralled by dyeing and experiment with a great variety of plants for colour will find

A home-spun shawl and coat made of Jacob's wool are modelled beside the wheels which produced their yarn. (Jill Goodwin.)

Opposite: A coat, hat and bag made entirely of woad-dyed wool by Enid Tivey. (Ray Harwood.)

100

Before and after: the beautiful cardigan on the right was made from the wool of this half-bred Suffolk sheep. (Enid Tivey.)

that samples accumulate rapidly and creep all over the house unless some kind of storage system is evolved. I make all kinds of baskets and containers from our home-grown rushes and willow to store my yarns and balls of wool before they are woven or knitted up.

Home-dyed yarns are very decorative and make bright patches of colour when dotted about the house on shelves or in dark corners. One dyer I know uses them instead of flowers as decoration, and another stores her hanks on a concertina-shaped clothes horse. Wool should be examined frequently for moths, which sometimes attack dyed yarn with great ferocity. Twenty-four hours in a bag inside the freezer will effectively kill off both moth eggs and grubs.

In a house which is largely furnished with products of the home dyepot I now have difficulty in remembering my own starting point in the constructions which clothe and upholster the family, but because my first large-scale dyeing was done in war time the wool was mainly used for jerseys, socks and warm hats. It has been said that if every loom in the world suddenly vanished we could still be warmly clothed with the products of our knitting pins and crochet hooks. It is possible to ply yarns together so that when they are knitted in certain stitches they are as closely textured as woven cloth. Many dyers do not realize that garments as well as cloth can be made without spinning. This is done by pulling out the fibres into finger-sized 'rovings' and giving them a slight twist as the knitting or crochet progresses. Garments can also be made from wool felt (see the instructions on page 21) cut into shapes and sown like woven cloth or quilted between layers of cotton or silk to make warm items like anoraks.

Long-stapled wools in particular, such as Lincoln longwool, Leicester and Wensleydale, lend themselves to the construction of garments without previous spinning. The fleeces are washed and dyed unspun and then teazed into long slivers of finger thickness. Because the longwool breeds have fleeces with such an exceptionally long staple the slight hand twist gives the necessary strength without making the fabric hard. Remember that the softest objects are made by this method, the next-softest by spinning with a hand spindle, and the hardest and most tightly twisted yarns by spinning on a wheel. It is good to experiment for yourself with all three methods in order to compare the tightness and elasticity of the different twists. I have made jerseys, capes, skirts, hats, cushions, shawls and rugs without spinning and they last and wear as well as clothes made by more conventional methods.

To use the unique yarns which you create by dyeing with natural materials it is worth searching for patterns and designs for clothes and furnishings which will enhance the beauty of your wools, silks or linens. These are best set off by plain and simple patterns consisting of traditional stitches and motifs, such as Shetland, Fair Isle, Aran and Icelandic knitting; Scandinavian braids for trimming garments; and patterns woven and cut from simple rectangles of cloth. 'Heirloom' shawls may be knitted or crocheted in a variety of shapes and sizes and these are particularly supple and soft when the wool has been spun on the hand spindle. Books such as *Cut My Cote*, *Simple Clothes* and *Clothes Without Patterns* (see the Bibliography) are particularly useful for garments of free design which will fit all shapes and sizes.

Ardent knitters may be content to use everything they dye, but others may wish to weave cloth or make rugs. For the beginner the best advice I can give is 'keep it simple'. There are many ways of making rugs without using large looms. The simplest of all is to knit or crochet squares or circles of very thick wool, blending the dyed samples carefully together and using them in stripes or blocks of colour. These may be backed for extra strength and wear with strong upholstery hessian, stout cotton or linen or smeared with an adhesive such as Copydex as a guard against slipping on polished floors. Many people do not like backing rugs as they say that dirt filters through and wears the rug by friction from the underneath. If the rug is washed after completion and squeezed gently in soapy water it will become compacted and firm enough to stand up to use without any backing.

Remember that the most beautiful rugs in the past have all been made with the simplest of looms and home-made hand tools, rigid poles to support the warp threads, and battens and combs for beating the pile. In the knotted oriental rugs there are from 150 to as many as 1,200 knots per sq. in., made with Persian or Ghiordes knots, and the dyes are all from plants or insects.

The more you become involved with making your own equipment the less you will enjoy using sophisticated mechanical tools. Today there is a real danger that the machine will take over from the craftsman and prevent him from freedom of expression by its limitations. I would far rather use a simple loom made from broomsticks as the supports and a heddle stick and batten for making the 'sheds' than an expensive foot-pedal loom which will make hundreds of complicated patterns by using different threading drafts. If you begin by using the simplest weaving equipment you will be able to decide as you gain experience just how complicated you wish your tools to become. A friend who has little space for craft equipment in her house spins all her yarns on a hand spindle and either knits or crochets her wool or weaves tiny 4-in. squares of cloth on a 9×6-in. picture frame. These she herringbone-stitches together to make garments which are both beautiful and unusual.

Your own equipment will depend on whether you spin, dye and weave for your own pleasure, or whether you wish to sell. I doubt very much whether a weaver today could make a living entirely by using primitive methods, because of the time factor, but it was not always so. Think of the thousands of hours which went to the making of a Persian carpet; how little the craftsman thought of time as the most important part of the operation (it was the least of his concerns); how much he wished his work to give delight and to endure for many years. The greatest rug makers were on a par with the cathedral builders and the creators of the Taj Mahal.

Pulling out a single lock from the fleece of a Lincoln Longwool to show the length of staple. (Jill Goodwin.)

From knitting, crochet and rug making we come to woven cloth and braids for the decoration of clothes or upholstery. To me, a homespun object must be either useful or beautiful, preferably both. I have always been too intent on making things which will be used continually for a long period of time to spare any thought for some of the more complicated and tortuous creations which not only seem monstrous and ugly but also fearful dust traps. The Navaho Indians combine beauty and utility in a very high degree with their hand-made blankets, rugs, saddle bags and wraps. They clip, dye, spin and weave the wool from their own sheep on simple frame looms which they make for themselves from logs and branches.

The finish of hand-made garments is very important and it is worth considering decorative stitches such as feather or faggoting for making joints and seams so that the stitching itself adds to the attractiveness of the garments.

In designing clothes made from hand-spun, naturally dyed wool, silk or linen choose timeless rather than high fashion styles. For example, the Celtic tunic, a rectangle of cloth with a round or transverse neck opening, either sleeveless or with elbow-length sleeves, requires the minimum of cutting and sewing. Two side seams and a neck edging are all that are required to finish the garment. Personally I very much dislike cutting homespun cloth at all because it tends to fray badly, but this can be prevented to a certain extent if it is stay-stitched on each side of the cutting line *before* cutting. Instead of shaping by cutting it is just as effective and far easier to shape with darts, pleats or folds at the bust, neck or shoulder. The Saxons and Normans were past masters at shaping their clothes in this way.

A crocheted scarf made from wool dyed with lichen (pink), willow herb (grey) and coltsfoot (green), worn with a home-made felt hat. (Monega Art Centre.)

Trimmings

From making our own knitting pins and crochet hooks from wood, bone and metal we may go a step further and create buttons and toggles as fastenings for our garments. Wood is comparatively easy to shape and drill and as only small pieces are needed it is possible to make a collection of beautiful wood from field and garden. Thick rose prunings cut into short lengths and left to season (one year per inch of thickness) make good buttons when cut and polished. Yew, maple, beech, birch, holly, oak and elm are all woods which polish well, and holly retains its whiteness after cutting. Long marrow bones, scrubbed and boiled before cutting, will also convert to buckles, toggles and buttons. Bone will polish like ivory if it is well rubbed with fine sandpaper and buffed with metal wadding. Keep a small saw and several files of different sizes for making fastenings, along with a miniature vice for holding the material while it is being cut.

Dye Charts

KEY TO SHORTENED FORMS
Chrome: *bichromate of potash*
Copper: *copper sulphate*
CT: *cream of tartar*
Iron: *ferrous sulphate*
Soda: *washing soda*
Tin: *stannous chloride*

Plants

COMMON NAME	LATIN NAME	PART USED	MORDANT	COLOUR
Acacia	*Acacia decurrens* *Acacia arabica* *Aria catechu*	Bark Pods	Alum No mordant	Yellow Orange-yellow
Ageratum	*Ageratum conyzoides*	Flowers	Alum Copper	Pale yellow Olive green
Agrimony	*Agrimonia eupatoria*	Whole plant	Alum Chrome Copper	Yellow Gold Green
Alder	*Alnus glutinosa*	Twigs Bark Fruit	Alum Chrome Copper	Yellow Gold Green
Alexanders	*Smyrnium olustratum*	Whole plant	Alum Chrome	Yellow Gold
Anatto	*Bixa orellana*	Seeds	Chrome	Orange
Anchusa	*Anchusa tinctoria,* *Alkanna tinctoria*	Roots	Alum & CT Acids	Red-brown Brighter reds
Angelica	*Angelica archangelica*	Whole plant	Copper Iron	Mid-green Darker green
Annual mercury	*Mercurialis annua*	Whole top	Infuse & ferment as for woad	Blues & blue-greens
Ash	*Fraxinus excelsior*	Fresh inner bark	No mordant	Yellow
Aster	*Aster amellus*	Flowers	Alum Chrome	Yellow Gold
Barberry	*Berberis vulgaris*	Stem Roots	Vinegar or acetic acid	Yellows
Bearberry	*Arctostaphylos uva-ursi*	Fruits	Vinegar or acetic acid	Blue

COMMON NAME	LATIN NAME	PART USED	MORDANT	COLOUR
Bilberry	*Vaccinium myrtillus*	Fruits	No mordant Salt Acids	Pinks Blue to grey Dark red
Bird cherry	*Prunus padus*	Bark	Alum Iron	Yellow Brown
Blackberry	*Rubus fruticosas*	Shoots Roots Leaves Berries	Iron Copper Alum & vinegar	Greens & grey Mid-green Pinks
Black walnut	*Juglans nigra*	Nuts Leaves Catkins Bark	No mordant	Rich browns
Blackcurrant	*Ribes nigrum*	Fruits Leaves	Acids Iron	Pinks & greys Greens & greys
Bloodroot	*Sanguinaria canadensis*	Fresh roots	Alum Tin	Red to orange Pinks & reds
Bog myrtle	*Myrica gale*	Leaves, fresh or dried	Alum	Yellow
Bracken	*Pteridium aquilinum*	Tops Shoots	Alum Chrome	Yellow green Warm green Grey on silk
Broad beans	*Vicia faba*	Stalks	Chrome Copper	Yellow-green Greens
Broom	*Genista tinctoria*	Tops	Alum & CT	Yellow
Bryony, white	*Bryonia dioica*	Berries	Oxalic acid or vinegar	Purple
Buckthorn	*Rhamnus frangula* *Rhamnis cathartica*	Berries Bark	Alum Iron	Yellow Deep brown
Buckwheat (ammonia-sensitive)	*Fagopyrum esculentum*	Whole plant	Alum Chrome Copper	Yellow Silver-green Olive green
Burdock (ammonia-sensitive)	*Arctium lappa*	Tops Leaves	Copper Copper & Iron	Orange-browns Deep brown
Bur marigold	*Bidens tripartita*	Tops Leaves	Alum No mordant	Orange-yellow Brilliant orange

COMMON NAME	LATIN NAME	PART USED	MORDANT	COLOUR
Camomile	*Anthemis tinctoria*	Flowers	Alum & CT	Bright yellows
Cardoon	*Cynara cardunculus*	Tops Leaves	Copper Iron	Greens Dark greens
Centaury	*Chlora perfoliata*	Tops	Alum & CT	Yellow
Carrot	*Daucus carota*	Tops	Alum Chrome Copper	Yellow Bronze Green
Chrysanthemum	Many types	Flowers	Alum Copper	Yellow Green
Sweet chestnut	*Castanea sativa*	Bark Twigs	No mordant	Browns
Horse chestnut	*Aesculus hippocastanum*	Nuts	No mordant	Browns
Chicory	*Cichorium intybus*	Leaves	Copper & soda	Rich burnt orange
Cleavers (goosegrass)	*Galium aparine*	Roots (*Only simmer — never boil*)	Alum & CT Tin	Red Bright red
Coffee	*Coffea arabica*	Coffee grounds	Alum & CT Iron	Browns & buffs Grey
Comfrey	*Symphytum officinale*	Tops Leaves	Copper Iron Copper, Iron & CT	Olive green Brown Dark greens
Coreopsis	All types *Coreopsis tinctoria*	Flowers	No mordant Alum Tin Chrome Iron & soda	Yellow Bright yellow Orange Bronze Reds
Cutch	*Acacia catechu*	Heartwood	Vinegar	Yellow
Cypress	*Cupressus sempervirens*	Tops Leaves	Chrome No mordant	Orange Brown
Dahlia	All types	Flowers	Alum & CT Chrome Tin	Yellow Orange Gold
Damsons	*Prunus damascena*	Berries	Vinegar or oxalic acid	Pinks, purple or blues

COMMON NAME	LATIN NAME	PART USED	MORDANT	COLOUR
Danewort	*Sambucus ebulus*	Berries	Vinegar, tin or oxalic acid	Purples
Dandelion	*Taraxacum officinale*	Flowers	Alum Tin or chrome	Bright yellow Oranges
Day lily	*Hemerocallis flava* & *H. fulva*	Flowers	Alum Tin Copper	Yellow Brilliant yellow Blue-green
Devil's bit scabious	*Scabiosa succusa*	Leaves	Fermented with soda	Blues
Dock	*Rumex* spp.	Leaves (early Feb.)	Chrome (early in year) Alum Chrome (later in year) Copper Iron	Reds Yellow Gold Green Darker green
Dog's mercury	*Mercuralis perennis*	Whole top	Alum, long fermentation	Buffs Brown
Dulse	*Rhodymenia palmata*	Whole plant	No mordant	Brown
Elecampane	*Inula helenium*	Root	Wood ash	Blue
Elder	*Sambucus nigra*	Leaves & twigs Fruit	Copper & Iron Vinegar or oxalic acid	Greens Blues & purples
Fat hen	*Chenopodium album*	Whole tops	Alum Copper	Dark green Bronze-green
Fennel (ammonia-sensitive)	*Foeniculum vulgare*	Tops	Copper Iron	Bronze-green Browns
Fenugreek	*Trigonella foenumgraecum*	Seeds	Alum & CT	Yellows
Fleabane	*Inula dysenterica*	Flowers	Alum & CT Chrome Copper	Yellows Oranges Greens
Floribunda rose	All types	Twigs Leaves Flowers	Alum Chrome Iron	Yellows Buff Grey

COMMON NAME	LATIN NAME	PART USED	MORDANT	COLOUR
Forsythia	*Forsythia* spp.	Leaves Shoots	Alum, CT & Iron	Deep green
Fuchsia	*Fuchsia magellanica*	Leaves Flowers	Vinegar or oxalic acid	Pinks & purple
Fustic	*Morus tinctoria*	Chips Wood	Alum Chrome Tin	Yellows Orange Gold
Geranium & cranesbill	*Pelargonium* spp.	Flowers	Vinegar or oxalic acid	Pinks, purple or grey
Globe artichoke	*Cynara scolymus*	Leaves	Copper	Greens
Goldenrod	*Solidago canadensis*	Flowers Tops	Alum Chrome Copper	Yellows Gold Bronze
Gorse	*Ulex europaeus*	Flowers	Alum Chrome	Yellow Gold
Gypsywort	*Lycopus europaeus*	Tops	Ammonia & iron	Rich browns
Heather	*Calluna vulgaris*	Flowering tops	Alum Chrome	Yellow Deep yellow
Hedge bedstraw	*Galium mollugo*	Roots	Alum & CT	Orange to red
Hemp agrimony	*Eupatoria cannabinum*	Tops (*only simmer — never boil*)	Alum Vinegar	Yellow Pink
Henna	*Lawsonia alba*	Tops	No mordant	Yellow
Holm Oak	*Quercus ilex*	Branches Leaves	Iron	Browns & greys
Hops	*Humulus lupus*	Tops Stalks	No mordant	Browns & reds
Horseradish (ammonia-sensitive)	*Armoracia rusticana*	Tops Leaves	Alum Chrome	Yellow Deeper yellow
Hornbeam	*Carpinus betulus*	Twigs Bark	Alum Chrome	Yellow Deeper yellow
Horsetail	*Equisetum* spp.	Whole plant	Alum	Yellow-green

COMMON NAME	LATIN NAME	PART USED	MORDANT	COLOUR
Horsetail	*Equisetum* spp.	Whole plant	Copper Iron	Green Deeper green
Iceland moss	*Cetraria islandica*	Whole plant	Alum Copper Ammonia	Orange Dark orange Brown
Indigo	*Indigofera tinctoria* & *I. suffruticosa*	Tops Leaves	Fermented with alkalis & bran	Blues
Iris	*Iris pseudacorus*	Roots Flowers	Iron Alum	Black Yellow
Juniper	*Juniperus communis*	Berries Tops	Alum & CT Alum & CT	Olive brown Purple-brown
Lady's bedstraw	*Galium verum*	Roots (*only simmer never boil*)	Alum & CT Chrome Iron	Orange-reds Reds Purple-reds
Lichen	Many species (see Chapter 10) Certain species	Whole plant	No mordant Ammonia & soda	Yellows, browns & oranges Reds & pinks
Lily-of-the-valley	*Convallaria majalis*	Leaves	Chrome Copper	Olive green Greens
Loganberry	*Rubus logonabaccus*	Leaves Fruit	Chrome Copper Iron	Olive green Deep green Brown
Logwood	*Haematoxylon campechianum*	Heartwood	Iron Alum Tin Chrome	Dark grey Violet-grey Purple Black
Madder	*Rubia tinctoria*	Roots (*only simmer — never boil; use hard water*)	Iron Tin Alum Chrome	Brown Scarlet Red Red-brown
Marigold	*Tagetes* & *Calendula* spp.	Flowers	Chrome Alum Copper	Orange Yellow Green
Masterwort	*Astrantia major*	Whole top	Alum Copper Iron	Yellow Green Dark green

COMMON NAME	LATIN NAME	PART USED	MORDANT	COLOUR
Marjoram	*Origanum majorana*	Whole top	Alum Chrome	Green Olive green
Meadowsweet	*Filipendula ulmaria,* *Spiraea ulmaria*	Whole tops	Iron Chrome	Brown Brown to grey
Mulberry	*Morus nigra*	Leaves Bark Fruit	Alum Chrome Acids	Yellow Orange to chestnut Greys & purples
Mullein	*Verbascum thapsus*	Whole tops	Copper Iron	Green Dark green
Northern bedstraw	*Galium boreale*	Roots (*only simmer —* *never boil;* *use hard water*)	Alum & CT Chrome Tin	Bright reds Deep reds Scarlet
Oak	*Quercus robur,* *Q. rubra*	All parts Acorns	No mordant Alum Copper	Browns Brown Olive green
Onions	*Allium cepa*	Outer skins	Alum Chrome Tin Iron	Yellow Orange Bright orange Browns
Peach	*Prunus persica*	Twigs Leaves	Alum Chrome Copper	Yellow Gold Green
Pear	*Pyrus communis*	Twigs Leaves	Alum Chrome Copper Iron	Yellow Gold Green Brown
Persian berries	*Rhamnus* spp.	Unripe fruit	Vinegar & tin Oxalic acid	Purple Violet
Persicaria	*Polygonum* spp.	Tops	Alum Chrome Copper	Yellow Gold Green
Pepperwort **(very ammonia-** **sensitive)**	*Lepidium campestre*	Tops	Copper Chrome Iron	Green Bright orange Deep brown
Plum	*Prunus* spp.	Leaves Twigs Fruit	Alum Chrome Acids	Yellow Orange Purples & greys

COMMON NAME	LATIN NAME	PART USED	MORDANT	COLOUR
Pokeweed	*Phytolacca americana*	Fruits	Alum Acids Soap	Reds Dark reds Grey-blue
Poplar	*Populus nigra*	Leaves Twigs	Iron Chrome Tin	Grey Gold Brown
Privet	*Ligustrum vulgare*	Leaves	Alum Chrome Copper	Yellow Orange Green
Queen Anne's Lace	*Daucus carota*	Tops	Alum & CT Tin & CT Copper	Yellow Orange-brown Green
Quercitron	*Quercus nigra,* *Q. tinctoria*	Inner bark	Alum & CT Tin With indigo	Yellow Orange Greens
Ragwort	*Senecio jacobaea*	Tops	Alum & CT Chrome Copper Iron	Yellow Gold to brown Bronze to green Darker green
Raspberry	*Rubus idaeus*	Leaves	Iron Tin Alum	Grey Green-grey Buff
Red cedar	*Juniperus virginiana*	Foliage	Rubbing alchohol Acids	Reds Pink-reds
Redcurrant	*Ribes sativum*	Leaves	Alum & CT Chrome Iron	Yellows Orange Green to grey
Reed	*Phragmites communis*	Tops Flowers	Alum & CT	Pale greens
Rhubarb	*Rheum rhaponticum*	Leaves Stalks	Copper Alum Tin	Green Yellow Bright pink
Rhododendron	*Rhododendron* spp.	Leaves	Iron Chrome	Grey Brown
Rhus or sumach	*Rhus* spp.	Berries Twigs	Alum Chrome	Brown Orange-brown

COMMON NAME	LATIN NAME	PART USED	MORDANT	COLOUR
St John's wort	*Hypericum perforatum*	Flowers Stalks	Alum Tin Alum	Yellow Orange-red Brown-reds
Safflower	*Carthamus tinctorius*	Flowers	Alum Acids	Yellow Pink to red
Saffron	*Crocus sativus*	Stigmas of flowers	Alum & CT Tin	Yellow Brilliant yellow
Sage	*Salvia officinalis*	Tops	Alum & CT Chrome Copper Iron	Yellow-buff Darker yellow Green Green-grey
Salsify	*Tragopogon porrifolius*	Tops	Alum & CT Tin Chrome Copper Copper & Iron	Yellow Bright yellow Bronze Green-yellow Darker green
Sawwort	*Serratula tinctoria*	Flowers	Tin, Alum & CT	Brilliant yellow
Sloe	*Prunus spinosa*	Fruit	Alum Acids	Rose pink Dark pink
Snowberry	*symphoricarpus albus*	Leaves Twigs	Alum & CT Chrome Copper Iron	Green-yellow Dark yellow Grey-green Olive green
Sorrel	*Rumex acetosa*	Tops	Ammonia Chrome Copper Vinegar Ammonia & copper Ammonia & iron	Dark olive Dark yellow Green Pinks Foxy brown Olive green
Spindle tree	*Euonymus europaeus*	Twigs Leaves	Alum & CT Chrome	Yellow Dark yellow
Sunflower	*Helianthus annuus*	Seeds Flowers	Copper & chrome Alum & CT Chrome Copper	Blue-green Yellow Orange Olive green
Tansy	*Tanacetum vulgare*	Tops	Alum & CT Copper Iron	Yellow Green Dark green

COMMON NAME	LATIN NAME	PART USED	MORDANT	COLOUR
Tea	*Camellia sinensis*	Dried leaves	No mordant	According to variety Buffs Browns Pinks
Toadflax	*Linaria vulgaris*	Tops Leaves	Alum Chrome Copper Iron Ammonia & iron	Bright yellow Deep orange Green Deep green Deep brown
Tomato	*Lycopersicon esculentum*	Vines	No mordant Copper Alum	Brown-red Green Buff
Tormentil	*Potentilla* spp.	Roots	Chrome Iron	Brown-red Purple-red
Turmeric	*Curcuma longa*	Powdered plant	No mordant Chrome Tin	Orange-yellow Deep orange Bright orange
Walnut	*Juglans nigra*	All parts	No mordant	Browns
Water Lily	*Nymphaea alba*	Roots	No mordant Iron	Dark brown Black
Wayfaring tree	*Viburnum lantana*	Leaves	Alum & CT Chrome	Yellow Orange
Weld	*Reseda luteola*	Tops Stalks	Chrome & ammonia Alum & CT Alum & tin Copper, CT & ammonia Iron Tin & CT	Old gold Yellow Orange-yellow Superb green Fine moss green Bright yellow
Willow	*Salix fragilis,* *S. triandra,* *S. caprea*	Twigs Leaves Bark	Alum Vinegar Oxalic acid	Yellow Pink Rose pink
Woad	*Isatis tinctoria*	First-year leaves (*use soft water*) Second-year leaves	All alkalis Alum All alkalis	Blues Pinks Violets & grey
Yarrow (ammonia-sensitive)	*Achillea millefolium*	Whole plant	Copper Iron Oxalic acid	Dark bronze Deep olive green Deep moss green

COMMON NAME	LATIN NAME	PART USED	MORDANT	COLOUR
Yew	*Taxus baccata*	Wood Tops	Acids	Pinks, reds & orange-reds

Other Dye Material

NAME	DESCRIPTION	MORDANT	COLOUR
Cochineal	Dried insects (*Dactylopius coccus*)	Alum & CT Alum Tin Chrome Oxalic acid & CT Iron	Dark red Magenta Scarlet Purple Rose geranium Purple or deep grey
Kermes	Dried insects (*Coccus ilicis*)	Acids	Deep red
Terracotta clay		Alum	Browns

METRIC CONVERSION TABLE

1oz = 28.35g
1lb = 0.454kg
1gal = 4.546l

To convert °F to °C:
$x°F = \frac{5}{9}(x - 32)°C$

List of Plants
according to Colour Yielded

Plants Which Yield Red, Pink, or Purple

Anchusa
Bilberry
Blackberry
Blackcurrant
Bloodroot
Bryony
Cleavers
Damson

Elderberry
Fuchsia
Geranium
Hedge bedstraw
Hemp agrimony
Lady's bedstraw
Lichen, some species
Logwood

Madder
Mulberry
Northern bedstraw
Persian berries
Plums
Pokeweed
Tormentil

Red cedar
Safflower
Sloe
Sorrel
Willow
Woad, with hard water
Yew

Plants Which Yield Blue

Bearberry
Day lily
Devil's bit scabious
Elecampane

Indigo
Logwood
Yellow iris, roots

Sunflower, seeds
Sloe
Woad, with soft water

Blackberry
Elderberry
Red cabbage

Plants Which Yield Yellow or Orange

Acacia
African marigold
Ageratum
Agrimony
Alder
Alexanders
Anatto
Ash
Aster
Barberry
Bird cherry
Bog myrtle
Broom
Buckthorn
Buckwheat
Bur marigold
Camomile

Centaury
Carrot, top
Chrysanthemum
Coreopsis
Cutch
Dahlia
Dandelion
Day lily
Dock
Fenugreek
Fleabane
Floribunda rose
Fustic
Goldenrod
Gorse
Heather
Hemp agrimony

Henna
Hornbeam
Horseradish
Horsetail
Iceland moss
Iris
Lichen, some species
Marigold
Masterwort
Mulberry, leaves
Onion
Peach
Pear
Persicaria
Pepperwort
Privet
Quercitron

Ragwort
Redcurrant, leaves
Rhubarb
St John's wort
Safflower
Saffron
Salsify
Sawwort
Sorrel
Spindle tree
Sunflower
Tansy
Toadflax
Turmeric
Wayfaring tree
Weld
Willow

Plants Which Yield Brown, Buff or Bronze

Bird cherry	Cutch	Hops	Raspberry
Black walnut	Dock	Iceland moss	Rhododendron
Buckthorn	Dog's mercury	Juniper	Rhus
Burdock	Dulse	Lichens, some species	Sorrel
Carrot	Fennel	Loganberry	Tea
Chestnut	Floribunda rose	Meadowsweet	Toadflax
Coffee	Goldenrod	Oak, acorns	Water lily
Comfrey	Gypsywort	Pepperwort	Yarrow
Coreopsis	Holm oak	Ragwort	

Plants Which Yield Green or Grey-green

Ageratum	Dock	Masterwort	Rhubarb
Agrimony	Elder	Marjoram	Sage
Angelica	Fat hen	Mullein	Salsify
Blackberry	Fennel	Peach	Snowberry
Blackcurrant	Fleabane	Pear	Sorrel
Bracken	Forsythia	Persicaria	Sunflower
Broad bean	Globe artichoke	Pepperwort	Tansy
Buckwheat	Horsetail	Privet	Toadflax
Cardoon	Lily-of-the-valley	Queen Anne's lace	Tomato
Carrot	Loganberry	Ragwort	Weld
Comfrey	Marigold	Reed	Yarrow

Protected Plants

It is against the law to gather the following plants:

Alpine gentian (*Gentiana nivalis*)
Alpine sow thistle (*Cicerbita alpina*)
Alpine woodsia (*Woodsia alpina*)
Blue heath (*Phylladoce caerulea*)
Cheddar pink (*Dianthus gratianopolitanus*)
Diapensia (*Diapensia lapponica*)
Drooping saxifrage (*Saxifraga cernua*)
Ghost orchid (*Epipogium aphyllum*)
Killarney fern (*Trichomanes speciosum*)
Lady's slipper (*Cypripedium calceolus*)
Mezereon (*Daphne mezereum*)
Military orchid (*Orchis militaris*)
Monkey orchid (*Orchis simia*)
Oblong woodsia (*Woodsia ilvensis*)
Red helleborine (*Cephalanthera rubra*)
Snowdon lily (*Lloydia serotina*)
Spiked speedwell (*Veronica spicata*)
Spring gentian (*Gentiana verna*)
Teesdale sandwort (*Minuartia stricta*)
Tufted saxifrage (*Saxifraga cespitosa*)
Wild gladiolus (*Gladiolus illyricus*)

Poisonous Plants

Use the following plants with great care and always in special saucepans kept solely for dyeing — *never* in cooking vessels:

Alder buckthorn (*Frangula alnus*)
Baneberry (*Actaea spicata*)
Bittersweet *or* woody nightshade (*Solanum dulcamara*)
Black bryony (*Tamus communis*)
Black nightshade (*Solanum nigrum*)
Buttercup (*Ranunculus* spp.)
Columbine (*Aquilegia vulgaris*)
Common buckthorn (*Rhamnus cathartica*)
Cow bane (*Cicuta virosa*)
Darnel rye grass (*Lolium temulentum*)
Deadly nightshade (*Atropa belladonna*)
Dog's mercury (*Mercurialis perennis*)
Fine-leaved water dropwort (*Oenanthe aquatica*)
Fool's parsley (*Aethusa cynapium*)
Foxglove (*Digitalis purpurea*)
Fritillary (*Fritillaria meleagris*)
Green hellebore (*Helleborus viridis*)
Hemlock (*Conium maculatum*)
Henbane (*Hyoscyamus niger*)
Ivy (*Hedera helix*)
Lily-of-the-valley (*Convallaria majalis*)
Lords-and-ladies *or* wild arum (*Arum maculatum*)
Meadow saffron (*Colchium autumnale*)
Mezereon (*Daphne mezereum*)
Mistletoe (*Viscum album*)
Monkshood (*Aconitum anglicum*)
Privet (*Ligustrum vulgare*)
Spindle tree (*Euonymus europaeus*)
Spurge (*Euphorbia* spp.)
Spurge laurel (*Daphne laureola*)
Stinking hellebore (*Helleborus foetidus*)
Thorn-apple (*Datura stramonium*)
White bryony (*Bryonia dioica*)
Yew (*Taxus baccata*)

Bibliography

Dyeing techniques were specialized early in man's development and tended to be invested with mystery. In many cultures women were in charge of the dyepots and they passed on their skills verbally, as they still do today in primitive communities. The modern dyer, however, has a large range of text books from which to choose and may have difficulty in choosing the most useful in each field, whether plants or technique. In selecting a bibliography I have included a few of the oldest and most useful books with more recent publications and they cover a wide range of raw materials, the harvesting and preparation of thread, spinning, dyeing, weaving and fabric construction. As nearly all the books mentioned contain individual bibliographies, the reader will in time be able to select a great deal of further reading in any special field in which he or she may be interested.

Books of special interest are marked with an asterisk.

Identifying Plants for Dyeing

* Bolton, Eileen M., *Lichens for Vegetable Dyeing* (Studio Books, 1960).
* Brightman, F. H., and B. E. Nicholson, *The Oxford Book of Flowerless Plants* (Oxford University Press, reprinted 1974).
* Grieve, Mrs M., *A Modern Herbal* ed. by Mrs C. F. Leyel (Jonathan Cape, reprinted 1977).
* Keble Martin, W., *The Concise British Flora in Colour* (Ebury Press and Michael Joseph, 1965).

Dye Plants in Use Throughout the World

* Adrosko, Rita J., *Natural Dyes and Home Dyeing* (Dover Publications, 1971).
  Anderson, Beryl, *Creative Spinning, Weaving and Plant Dyeing* (Angus and Robertson, 1971).
  Bancroft, Edward, *Experimental Researches Concerning the Philosophy of Permanent Colours*, Vol. 1 (London, 1813).
  Bemiss, Elijah, *The Dyer's Companion* (Dover Publications, 1973).
* *Brooklyn Botanic Garden Record. Plants and Gardens*, Vol. 20, No. 3, 'Dye Plants and Dyeing'.
* *Brooklyn Botanic Garden Record. Plants and Gardens*, Vol. 29, No. 2, 'Natural Plant Dyeing'.
* Bruncllo, Franco, *The Art of Dyeing in the History of Mankind* (Phoenix Dyeworks, Cleveland, Ohio, 1978).
  Bryan, Nonabeh G., and Stella Young, *Navajo Native Dyes* (Lawrence, Kansas, 1940; available from Stella Young, Chilocco, Oklahoma).
* Castino, Ruth, *Spinning and Dyeing the Natural Way* (Evans Bros, 1974).
* Clarkson, Rosetta, *Herbs. Their Culture and Uses* (Macmillan, reprinted 1967).
* Dyer, Anne, *Dyes from Natural Sources* (G. Bell & Sons, 1976).
* Grae, Ida, *Nature's Colors* (Collier Macmillan, 1974).
* Hummel, J. J., *The Dyeing of Textile Fabrics* (Cassell, 1896).
* Hurry, Dr J. B., *The Woad Plant and its Dye* (Oxford University Press, 1930; now reprinted by Augustus M. Kelley, Clifton, New Jersey 07012, and distributed in Great Britain by Merlin Press Ltd, 3 Manchester Road, London E14).
  Jacobs, Betty E. M., *Growing Herbs and Plants for Dyeing* (Select Books, Tarzana, California 91356, 1977).
* Leadbeater, Eliza, *Handspinning* (Cassell and Collier Macmillan, 1976).
* Lesch, Alma, *Vegetable Dyeing* (David & Charles, 1974).

* Lloyd, Joyce, *Dyes from Plants* (information on New Zealand plants) (Kerslake, Billens and Humphrey Ltd, Levin, New Zealand).
* Mairet, Ethel, *Vegetable Dyes* (Faber & Faber, reprinted 1941).
  Partridge, William, *A Practical Treatise on Dyeing* (Pasold Research Fund Ltd, Edington, Wiltshire, reprinted 1973 from 1823 edition).
* Ponting, K. G., *A Dictionary of Dyes and Dyeing* (Mills and Boon, 1980).
* Rhind, William, *A History of the Vegetable Kingdom* (Blackie, 1877).
* Robertson, Seonaid M., *Dyes from Plants* (Van Nostrand Reinhold, 1973).
* Thurstan, Violetta, *The Use of Vegetable Dyes* (Reeves-Dryad Press, Leicester, reprinted 1975).
* Waldmer McGrath, Judy, *Dyes from Lichens and Plants* (information on dye plants in the Arctic Circle) (Van Nostrand Reinhold, 1977).
  Wigginton, Eliot, (ed.) *Foxfire 2* (Anchor Press, Doubleday, New York, 1973).
* Wills, Norman T., *Woad in the Fens* (published privately at 23 Park Road, Long Sutton, Spalding, Lincs, 1979).

Spinning and Weaving

* Avery Amsden, Charles, *Navaho Weaving* (1934; reprinted by Peregrine Smith Inc., Salt Lake City and Santa Barbara, 1975).
  Barker, June, *Making Plaits and Braids* (Batsford, 1973).
* Broudy, Eric, *The Book of Looms* (Studio Vista, 1979).
* Brown, Rachel, *The Weaving, Spinning and Dyeing Book* (Routledge & Kegan Paul, 1979).
* Chadwick, Eileen, *The Craft of Handspinning* (Batsford, 1980).
* Coates, Helen, *Weaving for Amateurs*, How To Do It Series, No. 24 (The Studio Publications, London)
  Duncan, Mollie, *Creative Crafts with Wool and Flax* (G. Bell & Sons, 1971).
  Duncan, Mollie, *Spin Your Own Wool and Dye it and Weave it* (G. Bell & Sons, 1968).
* Ellacott, S. E., *Spinning and Weaving* (Methuen, 1956).
  Emery, Irene, *The Primary Structures of Fabrics* (Textile Museum, Washington DC, 1966).
  Ingers, Gertrud, and Ernst Fischer, *Flamskvävnad* (tapestry weaving) (I.C.A. Bokförlag Västeras, 1977).
  Irish Linen Guild, *Irish Linen* (Belfast, 1937).
* Jackson, Constance, and Judith Plowman, *The Woolcraft Book* (Collins, 1980).
  Macdonald, Angus, *Simple Tartan Weaving* (Dryad Press, Leicester, 1952).
* Miles, Vera, *Weaving Patterns for the 2-Way Loom* (Dryad Press, Leicester, 1965).
  Montgomery, F. M., *Printed Textiles 1700–1850* (Thames and Hudson, 1970).
* Picton, John, and John Mack, *African Textiles* (British Museum, 1979).
  Redman, Jane, *Frame Loom Weaving* (Van Nostrand Rheinhold, 1976).
* Reichard, Gladys A., *Weaving a Navajo Blanket* (Constable, 1974).
  Robinson, Stuart, *A History of Dyed Textiles* (Studio Vista, 1969).
  Simpson, L. E., and M. Weir, *The Weaver's Craft* (Dryad Press, Leicester, 1939).
  Steel, Tom, *The Life and Death of St Kilda* (National Trust for Scotland, 1965).
* Straub, Marianne, *Handweaving and Cloth Design* (Pelham Books, 1977).
* Trotzig, Liv, and Astrid Axelsson, *Weaving Bands* (Van Nostrand Rheinhold, 1972).
  Weir, S., *Spinning and Weaving in Palestine* (British Museum, 1970).
* Znamierowski, Nell, *Weaving* (Pan Craft Books, 1967).
  The Setts of Scottish Tartans (Oliver and Boyd, 1950).

Making Rugs

Andrews Marinoff, Kathryn, *Getting Started in Handmade Rugs* (Collier & Macmillan, 1971).
* Collingwood, Peter, *The Techniques of Rug Weaving* (Batsford, 1968).
* Hinchcliffe, John, and Angela Jeffs, *Rugs from Rags* (Orbis, 1977).

Making Clothes

* Bruhn, W., and M. Tilke, *Picture History of Costume* (Zwemmer, 1956).
  Burnham, Dorothy K., *'Cut My Cote'* (Textile Dept, Royal Ontario Museum, Toronto, 1973).
  Hofstätter, Kirsten, *Everybody's Knitting* (Penguin, 1978).
* Lokrantz, Kerstin, *Simple Clothes* (Penguin, 1975).

* Morgan, Fay, *Clothes Without Patterns* (Mills & Boon, 1977).
* Thomas, Mary, *Mary Thomas's Knitting Book* (Dover Publications, 1972).
* Tilke, M., *Costume Patterns and Designs* (Zwemmer, 1956).

Fibres for Dyeing

* Bowen, Godfrey, *Wool Away* (Van Nostrand Rheinhold, 1974).
* British Wool Marketing Board, *British Sheep Breeds* (BWMB, Oak Mills, Clayton, Bradford, West Yorkshire, 1978).

  Crowfoot, Grace M., *Methods of Handspinning in Egypt and the Sudan* (reprinted by Ruth Bean, Victoria Farmhouse, Carlton, Bedford, 1974).
* Davenport, Elsie G., *Handspinning* (Craft and Hobby Book Service, P.O. Box 626, Pacific Grove, California 93950, 1964).
* Teal, Peter, *Hand Wool Combing and Spinning* (Blandford Press, 1976).

  The Weaver's Journal, Vol. III, No. 2, Issue 10 (entire issue on silk), October 1978 (Boulder, Colorado 80301).

List of Suppliers, Museums and Craft Organizations

For Information:

The Design Centre,
28, Haymarket, London SW1 4SU

For Books, Equipment, Information and Fibres:

Mary Eve,
Carters, Station Road, Wickham Bishops,
Witham, Essex

Susan Foster
9 Windermere Road, Kendal, Cumbria

Mrs S Grierson,
Mill Books, Newmiln Farm, Tibbermore, Perth
PH1 1QN

The Handweavers Studio and Gallery,
29 Haroldstone Road, London E18

Frank Herring and Son,
West Street, Dorchester, Dorset

For Spinning Wheels:

Anne and James Williamson, 159 Main Street,
Asfordby, Melton Mowbray, Leicestershire LE14 3TS

For Seeds and Dye Plants:

John and Caroline Stevens, Sawyers Farm, Little Cornard, Sudbury, Suffolk

For Dyestuffs, Equipment and Mordants:

Gill Dalby, Clovers, Church Street, Alcombe,
Minehead Somerset TA24 6BL

Suppliers of Fleeces and yarns:

The British Wool Marketing Board,
Oak Mills, Clayton, Bradford,
West Yorkshire

The Rare Breeds Survival Trust,
Market Place, Haltwhistle,
Northumberland

Other Merchants will be found in
Skinners British Textile Register, published yearly at RAC House, Lansdowne Road, Croydon.

Museums

The American Museum, Bath.
The Bankfield Museum, Halifax.
Holburne Museum, Pulteney Street, Bath.
The Museum of Mankind, Burlington Gardens, London.
The Museum of English Rural Life, Reading.
The Piece Hall, Halifax.

York Castle Museum, Tower Street, York.

Royal Scottish Museum, Chambers Street, Edinburgh.

Welsh National Museum, St Fagans, Cardiff.

The British Crafts Council Gallery, 12 Waterloo Place, London.

The British Crafts Council, 143 Earlham Street, Covent Garden.

For small advertisments see the current numbers of the *Weavers Journal* published by the Association for the Guilds of Weavers Spinners and Dyers, BCM9 63. London WC1N 3XX.

For technical advice on textiles consult The Shirley Institute, Didsbury, Manchester, England.

Wool Marketing organizations around the world include:

International Wool Secretariat, 6-7 Carlton Gardens, London SW1

Australian Wool Corporation, Wool House, 578 Bourke Street, Melbourne 3000.

New Zealand Wool Marketing Corporation, 18 Brandon Street (P.0 Box 3849) Wellington CL.

Wool Bureau of Canada Ltd, 2200 Yonge Street, Toronto.

National Wool Marketing Corporations, 10 High Street, Boston 10 Mass, USA.

Index

Page numbers in *italic* refer to the illustrations.

Acacia catechu, 60
achillea, 47
acorns, 24
Africa, 20, 70
Agave fourcroydes, 28; *A. sisalana*, 28
Agricultural Advisory Service, 19
alder fruits, 50
alexanders, 47
alizarin, 65
alpaca, 28
Altamira, cave paintings, 7, 51
Alti Mountains, 7
alum, as a mordant, 12, 32, 34–5, 38; with cochineal, 56; for cotton, 24; for linen, 26–8; with logwood, 58; with madder, 66; with quercitron, 60; with safflower, 59; with weld, 63
ammonia, to alter colours, 40, 46; as a mordant, 34; used with weld, 64
ancient dyes, 7, 51–66
angelica, 47
Angora goats, 28
Angora rabbits, 28
aniline dyes, 13, 52
apple wood, 48
Arabs, 64
Aria catechu, 60
Armenia, 54
Asia, 62, 64, 73, 76, 87
Asia Minor, 62
Assyria, 76
asters, 47
Australia, 55

Bacillus indigogenous, 74
Baeyer, Adolf von, 67
Bancroft, Edward, 10, 54, 55, 60
barberry bark, 24
bark, preparation, 40
Beales, Percy, 13
Beales, Rita, 13
bedstraw, 46, 64–5
beetroot, 48, 50
begonias, 47
berberis, 48
Beyerinck, M. W., 78

bichromate of potash, as mordant, 34, 35, 38; with cochineal, 56; for cotton, 24; with fustic, 60; with logwood, 58–9; with madder, 66; with safflower, 59; for silk, 24; with weld, 64
Bidens tripartita, 46
bindweed, 44
birch, 48
bistort, 44
blackberry, 24, 40, 44
Boehmeria nivea, 28; *B. tenacissema*, 28
Bombyx mori, 10, 22
'bottom' dyeing, woad, 78
bracken, 44
Bradford blankets, 20
bran, as a reducing agent, 69, 70, 72, 80
breaking flax, 25; 26, 27
brightening agents, tin, 36, 38
British Museum Science Laboratory, 79
broom, 46
buccinium shellfish, 52, 87
buckwheat, 46
bur marigold, 46
burdock, 44
Burma, 56

cabbage, 48
cactus, 55–6
Caesar, Julius, *De Bello Gallico*, 78
Cambridgeshire, 78
camel hair, 28
Campeachy, 58
Canary Islands, 87, 91
Cannabis sativa, 28
carbonate of soda, 69
carminic acid, 55
carrots, 47, 50
Carthamus tinctorius, 59
cat hairs, 28
catechu, 60
caustic soda, 72–3
cave paintings, 7, 51
Central America, 58, 60
chalk, powdered, 63, 65, 69
chamomile, 32, 47
charlock, 46

chicory, 47
China, indigo, 51, 70, 73, 74; lac, 56; plant dyes, 59, 60; silk, 11, 22
china grass, 28
Chlorophora tinctoria, 60
citric acid, 59
Cladonia impexa, 91
cleavers, 40, 46, 48, 65
Coccidae, 51–2; 55
Coccus ilicis, 52–4
cochineal, 40, 51, 52, 64; dyeing with, 54–6; mordants for, 35, 55; used with quercitron, 60
Colbert, Jean, 71
comfrey, 35, 40, 46
Compositae, 35, 40, 44, 59
Constantinople, 52
copper, as mordant, 32
copper sulphate, as mordant, 34, 35–6; for cotton, 24; with fustic, 60; with logwood, 58; for silk, 24; with weld, 64
Corchorus capsularis, 28; *C. olitorius*, 28
coreopsis, 47
coriander, 47
Cornwall, 91
Cotswold sheep, 15
cotton, mordants, 24, 36
'count' system, wool, 18
cream of tartar, used with mordants, 34, 35, 36; with cochineal, 56; with fustic, 60; with logwood, 58; with madder, 66; with quercitron, 60; with safflower, 59; for silk, 24; with weld, 63–4
Crocus sativus, 62
Cruciferae, 32
Cuba fustic, 60
Curcuma longa, 60; *C. tinctoria*, 60
cutch, 51, 60

Dactylopius coccus, 54–5
dahlias, 44, 47
daisies, 44, 47
damsons, 40
dandelion, 35, 44
Darwin, Francis, 78
de-gumming silk, 22–3, 38

125

Derbyshire gritstone wool, 17
Devon, 50, 91
dill, 47
docks, 35, 40, 46
dog hairs, 28
dog's mercury, 44
dress-making, 104–5
drying, plants, 40; silk, 23; wool, 22
Dutch East India Company, 77
dyer's broom, 63
dyer's greenweed, 63
dyer's knotweed, 73
dyer's mulberry, 60
dyer's woodruff, 46, 64–5

East Anglia, 17, 76, 77–8
Ecuador, 52
Egypt, 12, 59, 62
Egyptian privet, 62
elder, 35, 36, 40, 44; 37, 48, 49
elecampane, 47
Elizabeth I, Queen of England, 77
equipment, 29–31, 39, 43
Essex Show, 19
Ethiopia, 59
Evernia prunastri, 90

felt, 21–2, 98–9; 21, 49
fennel, 47, 50
Fens, 51, 71, 74, 77–8; 77
fermentation, indigo, 20, 31, 70, 72–3, 80; urine as agent of, 20
ferrous sulphate, as mordant, 20, 24, 29, 34, 35, 36, 38; for cotton, 24; with fustic, 60; with logwood, 58; with madder, 66; reducing agent for indigo, 69; with weld, 64
feverfew, 47
flavine, 60
flax, 25–6; 25–7
fleabane, 44
fleeces, *see* sheep; wool
flower heads, 35, 47
forsythia, 40, 47
France, 63, 65, 91
fruits, dyes from, 48–50
Fuller, Thomas, 79
fustic, 60

Galium aparine, 40, 48, 65; *G. boreale*, 64; *G. mollugo*, 64; *G. odoratum*, 65; *G. verum*, 64
gallic acid, 62
garden plants, dyes from, 47–50
Genista tinctoria, 63
German knotgrass, 54

Germany, 63, 71
Glaubers Salts, 43
goats, Angora, 28; Kashmir wool, 28
goldenrod, 47
goosegrass, 46, 48, 65
Gordon, Dr Cuthbert, 90
Gossypium barbdense, 24; *G. herbaceum*, 24
Graebe, 65
Grana tinctorium, 54
grease, removal from wool, 20–1
Greece, 51, 62
Grieve, Mrs, *A Modern Herbal*, 32, 40
gum, removal from silk, 22–3, 38

hackling flax, 25–6; 26
Haematoxylon campecianum, 58
hay boxes, 30, 72
heather, 46
hedge bedstraw, 46, 64
Hellot, 55
hemp, 28; 49
henequen, 28
henna, 62–3
hennotannic acid, 62
Holkham Hall, Norfolk, 19
honeysuckle, 47
horseradish, 44, 46
Hummel, J. J., 68
Hurry, Dr J. B., 79
hydrated sodium carbonate, 34
hydrosulphite vat, 84–6; 85
Hypogymnia physodes, 91

India, cotton, 11, 24; indigo, 20, 70, 74; 71; lac, 56; plant dyes, 51, 59, 60, 62; silk, 22
indican, 67, 78, 82
indigo, 11, 40; 45; ancient uses, 51; cultivation, 72; dyeing with, 68–9, 72–3; dyeing linen, 28; dyeing silk, 24; extraction, 68; fermentation, 20, 31, 70, 72–3, 80; sources, 67–8, 70–80; storage, 73–4; synthetic, 67, 86; used with fustic, 60; used with quercitron, 60
indigoferas, 67, 70, 78
Indigofera anil, 70; *I. agentea*, 70; *I. suffruticosa*, 70; *I. tinctoria*, 70, 72
indoxyl, 78, 80, 82
insect dyes, 51–8
International Wool Secretariat, 18–19
Ireland, 87
iron, as a mordant, 36, 56
Isatis indigotina, 76; *I. tinctoria*, 32, 76
Italy, 63, 64

Jacob sheep, 100
Jamaica, 58
Japan, indigo, 73, 74; silk, 22
Java, 60, 70
jute, 28

Kashmir wool, 28
Kendal green, 78
kermes, 51, 52–4, 55, 64
kermes oaks, 52–4, 55
knitting, 102–3
knotgrass, 44
Kurdistan, 62

lac, 51, 52, 56–8
Lady's bedstraw, 46, 64
Lakshadia chinensis, 56; *L. communis*, 56
lanolin, 20
Lascaux, cave paintings, 51
Lawsonia inermis, 62
leaves, dyes from, 47–8
Leconora tartarea, 90
Leicester sheep, 18, 102
Lepidium campestre, 40, 46
levelling dyes, 43
lichens, 20, 31, 87–91; 37, 40
Liebermann, 65
lime, slaked, 69
Lincoln green, 78
Lincoln longwool, 18, 102; 16, 104
Lincolnshire, 76, 78
linen, dyes, 28; mordants, 26–8, 36; preparation of flax, 25–6; scouring, 26
ling, 46
Linum usitatissimum, 25
Lithuania, 54
litmus paper, 31, 40
llama hair, 28
Lobaria pulmonaria, 91
logwood, 58–9, 60
Lonchocarpus, 70, 75–6; 75; *L. cyanescens*, 68, 75
lovage, 47

Madagascar, 60, 70
madder, 12, 40, 47; 45; ancient uses, 51, 64–5; 64; cultivation, 46, 65–6; dyeing with, 66; dyeing silk, 24; harvesting, 66; mordants, 36; preparation for dye, 48; reducing agent for indigo, 69; storage, 66
Mairet, Ethel, 13
Mairet, Philip, 13
Maldon salt, 62
Margarodes polonicus, 54
Marsden, Mr, 74

Marsdenia, 68, 74–5
Martin, W. Keble, *The Concise British Flora*, 32, 44
Mediterranean, 87, 91
merino wool, 18
Mexico, 52, 54–5, 60
Michaelmas daisies, 47
Middle East, 11–12, 62
mignonette, 63
Minorca, 64
mohair, 28
mordants, ancient, 12; for cotton, 24, 36; for linen, 26–8, 36; for silk, 23–4, 36, 38; types, 32–4; for wool, 34–8
Morris, William, 13
Morus tinctoria, 60
moths in wool, 17, 102
mulberry, silkworms, 10, 22
mullein, 35, 46
murex shellfish, 52, 87
musk ox, 28
Mythe, 76

Navajo Indians, 20, 34, 104
Nerium oleander, 74; *N. tinctorium*, 68, 74
Netherlands, 65, 90
nettles, as a dye, 44; spinning fibres, 28; 49
New Zealand flax, 28
Nigeria, 75; 75
Nopalea cochinellifera, 55
Norfolk, 17
Normandy, 63, 71
North America, 64, 70
northern bedstraw, 46, 64
Nucella lapillus, 52
nuts, dyes from, 40, 50

oak, dyes from, 36, 55, 60; as mordant, 32
oak galls, as mordant, 24, 32
Ochrolechia parella, 91; *O. tartarea*, 87, 90, 91; 88
oleander, 74
onion skins, 35, 36, 44
Opuntia, 55; *O. polycantha*, 55–6
Orkney, 90
Ovid, 78
oxalic acid, 34, 36, 38, 56

Palestine, 62, 74
pansies, 47
Parmelia omphalodes, 91; *P. parietina*, 90; *P. physodes*, 91; *P. saxatilis*, 90. 91; 40
parsley, 47
Parsons Drove woad mill, 78

Partridge, William, 56
Paul I, Pope, 52
Peacock, Elizabeth, 13
pear wood, 48
pearl ash, 34
peat, dyes from, 50
Pennines, soils, 50
peonies, 47
pepperwort, 40, 44, 46
Perkins, William Henry, 13, 52
Persia, 62
persicaria, 44; 48
Phoenicians, 51, 52, 87, 91
Phormium tenax, 28
plants, ancient dyes, 58–66; dyes from garden plants, 47–50; dyes from weeds, 44–6
Pliny the Elder, 64, 78
Plowright, Dr, 79–80
Poland, 54
Polo, Marco, 70, 78
polygonums, 31, 74, 78; *aviculare*, 73; *P. chinense*, 73; *P. perseciria*, 68; *P. tinctorium*, 67–8, 70, 73
Polygonaceae, 44–6
poppies, 47
potash, bichromate of, *see* bichromate of potash
potash, purified, 34
purpurin, 65

quercitron, 60
Quercus coccifera, 52–4; *Q. nigra*, 60; *Q. tinctoria*, 60
quicklime, 69
quivit, 28

rabbits, Angora, 28
ragwort, 44
ramie, 28
Rare Breeds Survival Trust, 15, 19, 97
raspberries, 40
records, test dyeing, 39
reducing agents, indigo, 69, 70
Reseda luteola, 63–4; 64
retting flax, 25
rhea grass, 28
Rhind, William, 58
rhododendron, 36
rhubarb, 38, 46
Rhus coriara, 62; *R. glabra*, 62; *R. radicans*, 62; *R. vernix*, 62
Rocella tinctoria, 87, 91
roots, dyes from, 48
rosebay, 74

roses, 47, 48
ruberthyric acid, 65
Rubia tinctoria, 32, 64
Rubiaceae, 46
rubian, 65
rudbeckia, 47
Rudenko, S. J., 7
rugs, 103; 57, 61
Rumex, 35
Russia, 54
rust, as mordant, 32

safflower, 24, 59, 65
saffron, 51, 59, 62
St John's blood, 51, 52, 54
salsify, 50
salt, as a mordant, 12, 32, 34
sample boards, 29–30; 29
Saracens, 24
saucepans, 29; test dyeing, 43
Scandinavia, 76, 91
scent, relation to colour in plants, 44
schools, dyeing in, 93–9
Scleranthus perennis, 54
Scotch Blackface sheep, 15
Scotland, indigo, 80; lichen dyes, 87–9, 90, 91, urine fermentation, 20
scouring linen, 26
scutching flax, 25; 26
Sea Island cotton, 24
sea snail, 52
seeds, dyes from, 50
Serratula tinctoria, 32
shearing sheep, 17–18
sheep, coloured fleeces, 40–3; fleece types, 15, 18; shearing, 17–18
shellfish dyes, 51, 52, 87
Shetland Islands, 90
shield louse, 52–4
shrubs, dyes from, 48
Siam, 56
Sidon, 52, 87, 91
silk, de-gumming, 22–3, 38; drying, 23; dyeing, 24; mordants, 23–4, 36, 38; sources, 22; washing, 23
silkworms, 22; 23
sisal, 28
sloes, 24, 40
soda, fermentation of indigo, 72–3, 84; as mordant, 34, 38; mordanting cotton, 24; mordanting linen, 26–8
sodium carbonate, 69
sodium hydrosulphite, 72, 73, 84–6
sodium metabisulphite, 31, 73, 83
soils, dyes from, 50
Somerset, 50, 76

sorrel, *94*; dyes from, 35, 40, 50; as mordant, 32, 38
South Africa, 55
South America, 20, 28, 55, 58, 64, 70
Southdown sheep, 18; *16*
Spain, 54–5, 58, 64
spinning, flax, 27; wheels, *19*; wool, 20
stalks, dyes from, 47–8
stannous chloride, as mordant, 20, 34, 35, 36; with fustic, 60; with logwood, 58; with madder, 66; with weld, 63, 64
storage, indigo, 73–4; madder, 66; plants, 30–1, 40; samples, 29–30; *29*; woad, 70, 82–3; *83*
Suffolk sheep, *16*
suint, 20
sulphuric acid, 59
sumach, dyes from, 36, 48, 62; as mordant, 24, 32
Sumatra, 70, 74–5
sunflower seeds, 50
sweet cicely, 47

tannic acid, 24, 34, 36–8, 62
tannin, 32, 40, 65
tansy, 44, 47
tartaric acid, 58
test dyeing, 39–43
Tewkesbury, 76
thermometers, 31
thistles, 47
Thurston, Violetta, 13
Tibet, 56
Tibetan goats, 28

tin, as a brightening agent, 36, 38; as mordant, 56
toadflax, 35, 44
tomato vines, 50
'top' dyeing, woad, 78
treacle, reducing agent for indigo, 69
Turks, 54
turmeric, 24, 60–2
Tyre, 52, 87, 91
Tyrian purple, 52

Umbelliferae, 47
Umbilicaria pustulata, 90
United States of America, cochineal, 55; cotton, 24; indigo, 73; lichen dyes, 91; oak dyes, 60; sumach dyes, 62; urine fermentation, 20; woad, 76
urine, for cleaning wool, 20; as mordant, 12, 32; reducing agent for indigo, 20, 69, 70, 72
Urticaceae species, 28

vegetables, dyes from, 50
vicuna, 28
vinegar, as mordant, 12, 32; preparation of plant dyes, 40

Wales, 87, 90, 91
walnuts, 44, 48, 50; *45*
water pepper, 46
water persicaria, 44
weaving, 103–4
weeds, sources of dyes, 44–6
weld, 40, 46, 60, 63–4; *64*

Wensleydale sheep, 18, 102
West Indies, 60
whelks, 52
willow, 32, 37; *45*
Wills, Norman, 78
woad, 11, 12, 44, 47; *11*, *37*, *40*, *45*, *48*, *49*, *96*, *101*; chemistry, 82; competition from indigo, 71; cultivation, 80–2; dyeing with, 74, 78–80, 83–6; *85*; dyeing linen, 28; fermentation, 20, 30, 31; harvesting, 82; *81*; history, 51, 76–8; *77*; as source of indigo, 67, 68; storage, 70, 82–3; *83*; used with fustic, 60
wood, fastenings, 105
wood ash, as mordant, 32, 83; reducing agent for indigo, 70
wool, 'count' system, 18; drying, 22; felt, 21–2, 98–9; *21*, *49*; fleeces, 15, 40–3; *16*, *18*; mordants, 34–8; preparation for dyeing, 20–2; sources, 15–17, 18–19; spinning, 20; *19*; structure, 18
Wool Marketing Board, 16–17, 18

Xanthoria parietina, 89, 90; *89*

yak hair, 28
yarrow, 46
'yolk', in wool, 20
Yorkshire, 78

zinc, 69